T0114650

Within Normal Range

a memoir

Amie Joy

BALBOA.PRESS
A DIVISION OF HAY HOUSE

Balboa Press books may be ordered through booksellers or by contacting:

Balboa Press
A Division of Hay House
1663 Liberty Drive
Bloomington, IN 47403
www.balboapress.com
844-682-1282

Because of the dynamic nature of the Internet, any web addresses or links contained in this book may have changed since publication and may no longer be valid. The views expressed in this work are solely those of the author and do not necessarily reflect the views of the publisher, and the publisher hereby disclaims any responsibility for them.

The author of this book does not dispense medical advice or prescribe the use of any technique as a form of treatment for physical, emotional, or medical problems without the advice of a physician, either directly or indirectly. The intent of the author is only to offer information of a general nature to help you in your quest for emotional and spiritual well-being. In the event you use any of the information in this book for yourself, which is your constitutional right, the author and the publisher assume no responsibility for your actions.

Any people depicted in stock imagery provided by Getty Images are models, and such images are being used for illustrative purposes only. Certain stock imagery © Getty Images.

Print information available on the last page.

ISBN: 979-8-7652-3127-2 (sc)
ISBN: 979-8-7652-3128-9 (e)

Balboa Press rev. date: 07/26/2022

Chapter 1

"The Catholic Church teaches that it is the continuation of the early Christian community established by Jesus Christ; that its bishops are the successors to Jesus's apostles, and the Bishop of Rome, also known as the Pope, is the sole successor to Saint Peter who was appointed by Jesus in the New Testament as head of ..."

Deacon Bob is giving us a CliffsNotes version of the history of Catholicism on my first day of RCIA.

Rite of Christian Initiation for Adults ... it says at the top of my paper. The ink looks worn and there are faint marks across the top of each page, a sign that this document hasn't likely been updated in more than a century, simply photocopied hundreds of times.

It's hard for me to believe that this class is full. I'm surprised at the astonishing number of people who are willing to give up every Tuesday and Sunday night to become a Catholic. Isn't this supposed to be a dying religion? The younger generations choosing no religion or "the outdoors" as their form of worship. Maybe all these people are marrying into the Catholic faith like me? I imagine that they have also been asked by their fiancé to convert because it's very important to their family (whom only attend mass on high holidays).

So here we are, sitting in the rectory of St. Vincent DePaul, an old and established church tucked away in one of the most desirable (code word for expensive) neighborhoods in Denver. It's 2000 and we have all survived the Y2K scare — not that it matters because the Catholic Church is old school and you sign up by walking into the Parish Office, meeting with a priest and filling out paperwork. Only checks are accepted as payment. I glance around the room and I think my theory holds. Everyone here must be in the same boat, here by obligation, not by choice.

It's a pretty even mix of men and women, all about my age. Mid- to late-twenties with a similar "I have no choice but to be here" glazed look in their eyes. All but one person —a woman. She looks older than the rest of the group. I'm 25 so everyone looks older to me. If I had to guess, which I usually guess wrong, she's probably close to 40. She's pretty. Her hair is long and red, pulled back into a neat bun. She's definitely into this; she's wearing a silver necklace with one of those saint pendants hanging from the chain. She's not even a Catholic yet. Still in training and she's already donning saint merchandise.

She's dressed well. Crisp white shirt, black pants and black boots with a chunky heel. They look a little out of style, circa "Friends," but she still looks put together. Only a handful of years, but it matters. She probably has a high-powered job — I guess advertising. She just has that look to her. Doesn't look like the creative type, she's too type A for that, but there seems to be a little bit of an edge. Maybe she's an account executive hired to keep the creative types in line. She's taking notes furiously in a black leather portfolio with a fancy looking pen. She also has a Bible open next to her half-drunk Starbucks cup. Looks like iced coffee. At 7:00pm? Maybe it's decaf, but I doubt it. I just get the vibe that she's the caffeine-around-the-clock type.

There is no engagement ring on her finger, so I guess Catholic by marriage is not her category. She is the only one asking questions so this confirms my suspicions. She will be the class star, a go-getter in the realm of religious education. No one forced her to come. She is here by her own will, actually happy to be sitting in this tiny room that smells of musty carpet and printer ink.

Secretly, I do, too. I complain about it to anyone who will listen, but deep down I'm excited to learn about the Bible and to be part of a religion — something I didn't do as a child and I longed for it. My sister and I would go with our friends and their families to church and we loved it. It felt exciting and, even though I wouldn't have been able to articulate this back then, it felt a little like coming home. We didn't know any of the songs or Bible stories so we were the "non-Christian home kids" at the Friday night youth group gatherings over pizza and root beer.

Sometimes I felt like an actor at these events, trying to fit into a mold that I didn't understand. I said "God bless you" to people even when they didn't sneeze. I was repeating what I saw and really just trying to fit in, to be the good person I was supposed to be. Maybe this is what they mean by "born again?" You need to re-learn how to speak and how to be in the world? Memorize Bible verses and volunteer a lot? Jamie and I didn't have a clue, but we didn't care. We were having fun.

We liked hanging with the kids who prayed before each meal and said "God bless it" when they stubbed their toes. We blended because we were timid and kind. No acting required there. While our softball friends were our closest, we liked to dip our toes into all the social groups, never really committing but ensuring that we were liked by all. Titles like homecoming queen and class sweetheart usually went to one of us, but we weren't the typical high school girls with crowns. Instead, we valued being liked and known as the nice girls.

It's probably strange for most people to understand why I talk about my childhood as a "we." Jamie and I were — and still are — inseparable. We function as a unit. Also, when you're the only set of identical twins that a small Midwestern town has ever seen, you kind of get celebrity status. Or maybe it's a weirdo status. We stood out. Everyone knew who we were, we were different than the rest but lucky enough to have another person who was EXACTLY like the other. We felt lucky to function this way. All decisions were joint ones and we rarely disagreed.

Oh boy, there she goes, Miss Catholic, raising her hand like she's getting brownie points. I mean, I'm all for being an over-achiever, but this is a little much. I desperately want to tell her to chill out, she's making me anxious. Like she sucks the fun out of everything trying to be perfect or something. "Hey lady, life is too short," I want to say.

But I don't. I shuffle through the stack of papers and the list of patron saints catches my eye. On the chalkboard (yes, chalkboard), Deacon Bob has written out our assignments for next week. One is to decide on a patron saint for confirmation. Saints are the celebrities of the Church. I'm a subscriber to "Us" magazine so this is a religious activity I can get behind.

Deacon Bob describes them as being part of our extended family. We choose a saint to pray for us, root for us to get to heaven. "This decision should be taken very seriously," he says, and I know he means it, his voice very loud and still.

"When you're researching the saints, choose one that resonates with you. One whose lifetime work inspires your own. When you find the one that will be praying over your life in the Church, choose one who makes you feel closer to God," he instructs the class.

I'm pretty sure that Miss Catholic has already chosen hers because she is miles ahead of all of us. It's probably the saint she wears around her neck. Anyway, I'm excited about this so I stay up late that night reading through all the saints, even referring to my Catechism of the Catholic Church book. I have tried to read it through a couple of times because Deacon Bob says it's a very important book that summarizes the beliefs of the Catholic faithful. I find it hard to believe that it's a summary as it is by far the thickest tome on my bookshelf.

I read all of the descriptions of saints and one keeps standing out to me: Saint Teresa of Avila, also known as Saint Teresa of Jesus, who was referred to as a mystic. I don't know what that means, but I feel connected to her in some way.

She wasn't named a saint until 40 years after her death in 1622. This sounds tragic to me. She lived a life that was scrutinized, a life of sacrifice and deep spiritual connection to God that no one understood at the time. She was different, she had wild ideas, wrote books that many regarded as "silly." I'm sure they used a different word in the 1600s but that's my takeaway from the text that's very religious-buzz-word heavy. She was a reformer in the Carmelite Order.

She was tough, a survivor, having lived through the Hundred Years' War and the Black Plague. She gave it all away and charged on anyway, despite the odds. I found one story about her.

I could relate to Saint Teresa, the "other" Teresa I would say to my fellow Catholic wannabes. Because, of course, we all talked about our saints like men talk about the NFL draft during our coffee breaks and, when I said Saint Teresa, everyone assumed I meant Mother Teresa

Of course, she's one of the greatest people to have ever walked the earth, but I chose the "other" Saint Teresa because I related to her. I get her and, in some very weird woo-woo way, I feel like she gets me, too.

She was charming and liked to be liked. As I read this about a saint, I was a little surprised that she was in the category at all, but it's why I was drawn to her so much. She's real. Teresa suffered because it was easy for her to slip into the worldly life and ignore God. There were times when she got caught up more in flattery, vanity and gossip than spiritual guidance. And she was convinced that she was a terrible sinner, which is why she chose a religious life in the end.

For years she hardly prayed at all "under the guise of humility." She thought as a wicked sinner she didn't deserve to get favors from God.

Hmmmm. That's interesting. I wonder how she even became a saint. I like her and can relate to her. I scratch "St. Teresa of Avilla" down on my paper and place it on Deacon Bob's desk at the same time as Miss Catholic. Our hands reach for the basket at the same time. We turn to look at each other in unison, our eyes meet. I blink and look harder for a new perspective, but she doesn't flinch. Her brown eyes that are really more auburn and match her hair are steady on mine.

Chapter 2

"OK," I say to myself for what is probably the twentieth time within the last five minutes. That's what I do when I'm nervous. I like to reassure myself by saying it's OK when I'm completely terrified and quite certain that nothing is OK. That, in fact, the floor is about to drop out from under me.

It's the first week of my new job. I'm a senior account executive at an adverting agency, assigned to the agency's biggest technology client. I'll be working solely with this client, helping them revamp their marketing and communications. I feel important yet minuscule at the same time as I step out of the taxi onto the busy Manhattan street to walk into my first meeting. I flew in on the 5am flight from Denver and am exhausted.

But my new suit is wrinkle-free and fashionable. My heels are high, although I feel tiny next to this intimidating building. I give myself the luxury of one more, "OK," take a deep breath and then I'm off, walking up the stairs and into the beautifully gold-lined glass doors. I see my overly big, toothy, smiling reflection.

And it was that moment, right there, that changed everything. I was still sleep walking, so I didn't realize it at the time. It took many years for it to hit me upside the head like a ton of bricks. But it was *that* moment.

The one where I made a choice to step into courage and it changed my life forever. I just thought, "Look at me, getting a job that

I'm not qualified for so I can make enough money to show everyone that I'm worth something, especially me." I had no idea that it would be the spark that ignited a fire inside me that would keep burning and getting so out of control that I couldn't contain it any longer. That light would overcome the darkness that swept me up at an early age.

My very first memory is a panic attack. At the age of five as I lie in my bed, my body stiff as a board, my heart pounding and a deep knowing that I just wasn't right. Not the same as everyone else. I felt scared, alone, dark. I was too young to comprehend what was happening to me at the time, but the feelings are etched into my brain and I was able to process it years later when I experienced the same terror. It was familiar to me and once I was old enough to name it, it was equally disturbing to know that I had encountered it at such an early age.

"OK," I say. This time in my head as I now stand in the corner alone in the crowded hotel bar, the meetings are now over and it's time to socialize and continue the work charade over drinks and dinner. Everyone is standing in small groups of three or four with drinks in their hands, conversation flowing about the latest stock prices and product launches.

I decide to walk around, make it look like I'm mingling, maybe jump in on the conversation that sounds friendly enough to join. No such luck. Acronyms are being thrown around like daggers and I have no idea what they mean. I'm one of five women in the room, by far the youngest, and I can feel that I will not be taken under the wing of a fellow female. Quite the opposite in this atmosphere.

I see them silently but violently sizing me up. Ready for their chance to pounce on something stupid I might say — and I have given them plenty to pounce on today. I tried desperately to keep to myself and avoid speaking my opinions. I'm usually quite good at this, able to hold a conversation and provide balance for others without giving up my view on the topic. Better to be silent and liked was my motto. But today, something was off. I listened to that quiet voice inside and actually gave her some time on the mic. And this was no small potatoes, I spoke up in front of more than 50 strangers who were staring at me blankly, wondering who the hell I was and what was I talking about.

The group was passionately discussing the lack of clear communications when I heard my voice raise to an octave that others might actually hear from across the room. I offered my advice, clearly stating that the team needed a defined communications plan that aligns across the business — one that's not siloed as it is today, but really collaborative. I even suggested that I work with each of the go-to-market executives to understand their individual needs so we can work in a way that is aligned for us and our internal audiences.

I was impressed. I sounded like I knew what I was talking about when, in reality, I had no idea. It was just an educated and anxiety-induced guess. The vice president of global sales, my main point of contact as a contractor, was satisfied with that, shaking his head, thanking me and asking his direct reports to "grab some time" with me and make it a priority. I slithered back down into my seat.

The rest of the day I sat through meetings about the new fiscal year budget, programs and products that are being launched and projections on the business. There was arguing, laughing and very lively conversation as I could feel the balance of power shifting each time a new presenter stood up and took control of the projector. Most of the day I sat quietly, taking notes tentatively. Sometimes even doodling on my paper to look busy and avoid the sideways glances when I was finally formally introduced as the "agency consultant" who would be working with the team to manage communications and marketing transformation.

I told myself, "OK" very gently in my overwhelmed brain and stood to give an introduction to my new colleagues. "Hello everyone," I gave a slight and silly wave across the room. Then I went on, "I'm Amie and I'm thrilled to be here with you all and learn about the business." I could have stopped there, but didn't. "It sounds like you have a very busy and impactful fiscal year ahead — wanted to throw in the lingo — and I think communications will be a critical tool to help us meet our goals. So I look forward to being part of it." I smiled, waiting for a "welcome" or maybe even a question, but there was silence among more than a few smiling faces so I sat down, grabbed my pen and started doodling away.

A new circle has just formed right by the bar where I'm standing so I decide to take a couple steps closer in hopes of inclusion. All eyes turn to me and my breath catches a little when I look up to see the most piercing blue eyes I've ever seen staring back at me. He's staring through me and his face looks, well, startled.

Did I say something offensive? I'm pretty sure I haven't even muttered a word ... yet. Oh, it's there on the tip of my tongue, if only I could choose one from the millions of thoughts per second that are firing.

He has obviously noticed me loitering outside this circle of suits. It's all men, and I'm used to it. I have worked in only two industries: finance and technology, both dominated and controlled by males. I've never minded. In fact, I feel that I work best with men. I find it easier to befriend them and not get too emotionally involved. It feels safer to me.

Now here I am again, one of five women in the room. But I stand out, no doubt about it. Among the dark suits, a muted range from dark gray, dark navy to black/black. I'm standing just outside of this circle wearing white boot-cut suit pants, a pale blue blouse and a white suit jacket. It's beautiful, fits like a glove and it's summer for God's sake. In my over-worked mind, it's much more appropriate than dressing like I'm going to a funeral. Maybe that's why he's staring? The white could be hurting his eyes or when I step within five feet of these dark-clad egos, maybe it's like a flashlight?

Or maybe it's like when you're driving at sunset and the sun is blinding you. "Sunshine delays" they call it in Colorado. It's one of those secrets that we Coloradans hang on to. The sun is so intense that you have to wear sunscreen year round and, even when it's 37 degrees, the sun is still beating onto your car so intensely that you have to turn on the air conditioning. People may come for the weed and mountain sports, but they stay for the sunshine.

This is just a taste of the thousands of thoughts that bounce around my very busy and crowded mind. That one, the whole bit about the sunshine, squeaked through at the last minute and talked my hands into typing fast enough to keep up. It's very hard to do and most of the time, the thoughts are so fast and frantic that my poor swollen, arthritic fingers just can't keep up. It's a battle to the end, my hands pleading with my brain, "please slow down or at least give me a minute to rest, even take a few seconds to put in the appropriate spacing, let alone punctuation." But the thoughts get agitated and pick up speed, getting a little smug. "Well, if you can't keep up, then you really need to get it together and haven't you heard of editing? You can add spacing and punctuation later in the next draft. This is important! I'm so sick of you holding us back."

"Hi there, Amie. It's Amie, right?" he finally speaks. A look of alarm still on his face. Now, I've heard of resting bitch face, I wonder if this is something similar. This man, who is handsome in a subtle, politician-with-power kind of way, may have resting "alarmed for no reason" face. I know, it's not a thing, but I'm coining it now and may even blog about it later to see if I can find other people who have encountered this "syndrome."

This is probably not the best time to ask him about it so I reply instead, "Hi. YES, it's Amie. Who are you?" way too eagerly, sticking out my hand to shake his. He takes my hand gently at first and then firmly and looks me directly in the eyes. More staring through me, but this time up close, which is unnerving. He had taken just a few steps so that he was only inches away from my face. Then after a very uncomfortable 10 seconds of silence (I was counting), he replies, "I'm Jonathan, it's so nice to finally meet you."

He lets go of my hand and takes a step back, undoubtedly sensing my discomfort and I notice that the social circle has now dismantled, the other men who were standing here are now part of the greater sea of dark suits. That was quick, they must have been looking for an opportunity to leave the conversation. With this guy's level of intensity, I can see why. It's not that he's boisterous or loud, but his presence is strong, almost intimidating. But I can sense right away that he's interesting, something there that I want to understand more.

"Welcome to the team. I understand this is your first week in the role," he sort of asks, sort of states. He continues when he sees that I'm not going to respond, possible answers and topics of conversation still crowding my head.

"So, from whom did we steal you away?" he asks.

Although it was a strange way to ask, I'm guessing that he wants to know where I was working before. I hesitate, choosing my words carefully, "Well, I owned my own business, a small advertising agency in Denver, so I guess you could say you stole me away from … myself." He likes this answer very much. Although there is just the hint of a smile starting to form on his face, I can see the amusement radiating from his eyes.

"Well that's fascinating, tell me more," he smirks, the expression resembling a smile on his olive colored, chiseled face. So I go on and on talking animatedly with my hands about the small business clients that I worked for, how I would build brands and create marketing plans for local restaurants, retail stores, that kind of thing.

I hear his laugh for the first time, more like a giggle, when I tell him that I once traded my marketing services for yoga classes. Because I was so busy writing website copy and communications while taking care of my young kids at the same time, I didn't have time to go to the yoga classes. And then when I finally showed up to a class a month later, the owner said blankly, "Sorry, your free class pass has expired."

I did this a lot, working long hours for very little to no pay. I really didn't mind much, although the yoga trade did sting a little. It was very hard to take deep, cleansing breaths every time I stepped my bare feet into that studio. I loved the creativity and the satisfaction of helping a small business get their start and grow. I helped them put something beautiful into the world. But it was most certainly not all me. "Caroline," I told Jonathan, "was my business partner and the creative brains of the operation."

My excuse was that I was trying to build my business and these things take time and so what if I didn't turn a profit the first few years, "I'm sure this is standard," I would constantly reassure my husband. He never agreed, just rolled his eyes and made comments like, "Well, free doesn't buy groceries and free doesn't pay for all your small Target purchases that add up." Of course he was right, but I was convinced that things would turn around. Half glass full kind of thinking. I was sure the positivity would win in the end.

Then I would slink back to my office after I put the kids to bed to work into the wee hours. "Work harder," I would think. "Work smarter," I would promise myself and I was convinced that this was the way to have the best of both worlds.

My theory was a good one. I would build my business while my girls were young, work hard during their naptimes and after bedtime. And all the moments in between they would be by my side as I made calls to customer prospects and set up photo shoots. I would strap them into their car seats and drive downtown for meetings with printers and my business partner.

As I prepare to launch into a story about changing diapers while on conference calls, a bell rings and I see everyone shuffling out of the room, to the dining room I assume. Saved by the bell, literally.

Why on earth did I think that it was a good idea to share all of this irrelevant and ridiculous banter? This was my out and I sighed in relief — out loud, of course, as if the last 11 minutes weren't embarrassing enough.

He's polite, still smiling his half smile and a sparkle in his eye, he reached for my hand again. "It has been an absolute pleasure to meet you and to learn a little about you," he says, and it feels genuine. Then he looks at me in the eyes again, with even more intensity and says, "I hope that I will have the pleasure of talking with you more tonight and I'm honored that you have decided to join our little company. We have big shoes to fill for you." And then he was off, swept up in the sea of suits.

I take my time going into the dining room. I check my phone for texts, emails, take a quick look on Facebook when there were no new messages anywhere else. Then I call the house but it goes to voicemail.

"Hi guys! Two more sleeps then mommy will be home to tuck you in, I love you, goodnight," I say in a hushed voice so no one else overhears. I don't want anyone to think I'm unprofessional.

Finally, I work up the courage to walk toward the buzz of pre-dinner conversation. The room is beautiful. A ballroom. A fancy one with giant gold and crystal chandeliers dripping from the ceiling. Tall windows overlook South Central Park and I see the shadows of people walking by, a horse and carriage in the distance. I imagine all the speeches from maids of honor, awkward applause as a groom smashes wedding cake into the face of his new bride. Glasses clinking, encouraging the newly married couple to honor their guests with a public display of affection. My imagination getting carried away, I can almost hear the chicken dance, taste the wedding cake.

But I'm quickly reminded that I'm not here for a wedding when I see Sam stand up, lightly tapping his glass with a fork and the conversations quiet to a low hush. I'm the only one standing so I scan the room for an open seat. I don't see one. My heartbeat is starting to pick up speed as I run/walk across the room toward the front where I see one empty chair.

I slide into the chair that's elegantly upholstered in a thin tan and white chevron patterned material with gold piping. It feels like silk, I notice, as I try to sidle my way into the chair without pulling it out from under the white linen-draped table. I'm small enough, but I bang my knee on the table and I hear the glasses moving and silverware shifting. I'm too mortified to look around the table so I keep my eyes focused on my boss as he thanks everyone for being here and for all of their hard work this quarter.

"I especially want to thank Jonathan Nelson for taking time out of his crazy schedule to be here. Jonathan, we're grateful for your continued leadership as an active principal and co-founder." Then, I feel everyone's eyes on me and I start to flush.

"Why are they looking at me?" I think and then I finally look around the table and there's Jonathan, sitting just to my left. The crowd applauds and he nods his head in acknowledgment and mouths a humble, "thank you."

The applause dies down as Sam continues on with his speech. I'm still looking at Jonathan, stunned that he seems to be the most important person in the room and even more surprised that I chose him out of all of the suits filling this room to bore with my ridiculous stories. Even worse, I have told him in detail about my background, so I've outed myself as completely unqualified for this new job that I'm desperate to keep.

He catches me staring and gives me a knowing wink and this time a bigger smile, both sides of his pencil-thin lips curving and he giggles then turns back toward the stage.

Finally, the speech comes to an end. Nearly everyone in the room is acknowledged for something. In my opinion, it's very "everyone gets a blue ribbon" kind of behavior. More likely that this guy, my new boss, is the type that doesn't like to rock the boat. Good for me, I think, sure that's it's a good sign for job security. He talks about what he needs everyone to do for "a successful quarter."

As the salads arrive, conversation is picking up around the table and I finally have the courage to look up from my phone, where I have been scrolling, glancing down every few seconds to look very busy and important and so that no one will talk to me. No such luck as I hear the chair to my left scooting closer to me and then, "Lucky me that I get to sit next to you. We can continue our conversation," Jonathan says quietly, very close to my right ear I notice. I feel eyes on me again and this time I'm right. The woman sitting across from me says, "Interesting, the only seat left in the place and it's for you. The new girl gets to sit next to the boss." "Brave girl," she adds, quite bitchy really.

There are introductions. The guy to my right with the sweet smile and slight southern accent starts it up. "Joe Murphy, so nice to meet you. I'm excited to work with you," he says and then he pours me a glass of red wine. I can tell that we will be friends right away.

I don't like red wine, but I don't say anything; I just smile and we clink glasses. Then, there is a silent understanding that everyone will follow suit. I nod and smile, waving, then mouthing "hi," and "nice to meet you" as people politely state their name and role and then quickly pass the invisible baton on to the next innocent bystander.

Jonathan introduces himself as co-founder of the company and then it's back to me. I just smile shyly and say, "I'm Amie, luckily I get a pass since I introduced myself to everyone this morning. Unless no one was paying attention?" Then I laugh generously. But when no one joins me in the laugh, I just stop talking abruptly, pick up a fork and start shoving salad into my mouth.

I'm saved next by the waitress asking me if I would like a drink. Thank God, I think. I quickly scan the wine menu that's sitting between me and Jonathan. I strain my neck to read it then look up at the waitress. I immediately like her. She's smiling and it seems genuine, probably the only genuine smile I've seen since the flight attendant that gave me an extra blanket on my early morning flight. "I'll have your house white wine please?" I ask like she might say "no." She smiles then takes the other orders that are being shouted at her. Everyone is getting a little tipsy — the volume of conversation has gone up a few octaves over the last half hour as everyone is on their third or fourth drink before dinner arrives.

Jonathan leans over and we talk non-stop, covering everything from where we're from to our favorite books. The conversation is easy, flowing like the cocktails and wine that are flowing around us. For the first time since I got here I'm not focused on the people around me, the noise and expectations slip away. I can feel eyes on me again so I lift my head for a quick scan around the table, hoping no one will see. Oh, they see, as everyone is looking at us, but as soon as they meet my eyes they look away, embarrassed that I've caught them.

I have no idea what they're thinking but I wonder if they can feel the energy that I can feel. There is something special here, bouncing between Jonathan and me. I don't know what it is, but it feels so comfortable and I realize that this is the first time in a very long time that I'm acting like myself, saying the things I want to say and my insecurities are nowhere to be found. I'm certain they're there somewhere, they never stray too far. But on a rare occasion they will walk away and give me some space. I hope that I can keep the distance this time, find a way to evict them out of my head for good. But, I'm a realist and try to keep my expectations low. I will just enjoy this little break for now and make the most of it.

I turn back to him and blurt out, "I feel like I've known you forever." I'm not sure why I say it, but I know it's true as soon as it slips out of my mouth. I spend the next 10 minutes drilling him with questions, a not-so-subtle way to determine if we've actually met before, which feels like a real possibility. He's patient and considerate, answering all of my questions with the amused look still plastered on his face.

When I haven't found a mutual friend or relative that we might share, I ask, "OK, so what's your nationality?" He says American, but then answers seriously, "I am the worst possible combination," he pauses for effect. Then through a true smile this time, he says, "Irish and German." I can still feel eyes on us and know that I should bring others into the conversation, but I ignore the pull and keep my focus here on this little bubble of fun and safety that we've created.

"What?!" I say, laughing so hard that I'm dangerously close to snorting. Now, even though my insecurities are taking a little break, I still wouldn't allow myself to snort in front of anyone, let alone my work colleagues. "Well, now that's quite an insult, I'm Irish and German, too. But I must admit, it *is* the worst combination. When you consider skin cancer risk, alcoholism and emotional paralysis caused by deadly dictators," I go on, thinking I'm very funny at this point. He's laughing too and I can feel eyes intensify on us.

"Well, now we understand the ease in our conversation, we have the same genetic makeup for the craic and being totally rude and leaving everyone else out."

Then he eloquently leans to his left and brings Mary into our conversation. After just a few minutes, three others have joined in our now very different but still pleasant dialogue.

I watch him as he orchestrates the table, pulling people in with his charm. He has mastered the dance of conversation. I see him listening with his eyes, only interjecting when it's absolutely necessary. His responses are crisp and calculated, commanding respect and likeability.

He's not wearing a wedding ring I notice. Why did I notice that?

There are now a few pockets of lively conversation popping up around the table, people making connections, telling stories about their travel to the countries everyone has mentioned. Jonathan notices too, nods his head in approval and turns back to me, picks up his fork and taps my white wine, only a few sips missing.

"What's your drink of choice?" he asks. I shrug, pick up my glass and take a sip before answering, "Just the house white wine," I say as I force it down, it's sweet with an after taste that makes my throat burn a little. I want to cough, but I push it down with another sip.

"Well," he says, smiling and grabbing the wine menu. He pushes the menu further from him, toward the table as he strains his eyes to see. I haven't asked how old he is, but by the way he's struggling to see the menu, I'm guessing over 40. I hear that after 40 is when the "cheater" glasses come into play.

He scoots his chair closer to mine and puts the menu in front of me, pointing to his selection: Pascal Jolivet 2009 Indigène (Pouilly-Fumé). I can't pronounce it so I just say, "Great, looks good," even though I see right away that it costs $82 per bottle and there is no by-the-glass option. He raises his hand, waving the waitress over and says, "we'll have a bottle of the Pascal Jolivet and a fresh glass for the lady, please."

I'm impressed, not only by his beautiful pronunciation of the very French name, but also by the way he confidently made the gesture. It made me feel special, like he was taking care of me. Plus it was very sexy, I thought. I was flushed with guilt at that thought, but decide this is no time to start down my neurotic path and make the decision to go with the flow here. The wine flowed and so did the conversation.

Together, we finish off the very delicious bottle of wine and I finally admit to him that it went down much smoother than the house wine I started on.

We laugh about our shared aversion to plaid and people who don't turn left at yellow lights. We share about our childhoods, exchange most embarrassing moments and I even tell him about my habit of jumping on stage at concerts and my self-proclaimed title of "musical marvel" when I've had a few drinks. This feels more like a first date than a work dinner.

He finds it hysterical when I order chicken marsala, then I overshare that I only ordered it because the character in the book I was reading ordered the dish on an anxiety-ridden date with a sexy lawyer who was representing her case.

"Pride and Prejudice is my favorite book," I tell him when he asks about what I like to read. More first-date like questioning.

Chapter 3

Back in my quiet, dark hotel room, I sit on the plush king sized bed and I feel stunned. I'm not sure what has happened to me, but something deep within has changed. Do I feel elated or terrified? I can still feel Jonathan's presence, his eyes, his energy blaring into me. I'm unsteady, shaking a little, but I feel a joy and lightness that I've never encountered.

Surely there is something wrong with me. This is not the way a married woman of 10 years and mother of two should feel. I don't turn on the TV, like I usually would. It's my effort to add some noise to drown out my thoughts on the rare occasions when I'm alone. Instead, I sit in the stillness for what feels like a very long time. When I finally look at the clock it's 2am. I don't bother to change into my pajamas or wash my face, I just scoot up to the top of the bed and pull the covers up to my chin.

Jonathan's the first person I see as I pick up a plate at the breakfast buffet. "Good morning," he says, his smile big this time. I can feel my neck flush and my hand goes to my throat automatically. "Good morning," I reply, looking down the line of silver trays, filled with fluffy eggs and crispy bacon and I decide to focus on breakfast rather than what's happening in my body.

Halfway through the day, he finally walks over, takes the seat next to me and moves in close. In between speakers he says in a very low voice, almost a whisper, with eyes still on the spot at the front of the room where the next presenter is setting up his laptop, "Well, meeting you sure was unexpected." The presenter is plugging cords into his laptop and banging on his keyboard in frustration as Jonathan continues, "So the only conclusion I can come up with is that we knew each other in another life." Then he looks at me. I'm speechless and, when he realizes that I'm not going to respond, he stuns me some more, "I couldn't sleep last night, I just sat there in the dark thinking about how astonishing it was to meet you, like I was struck by lightning or something. But it was more pleasant than that, not like I have brain damage or was shocked. I would say that I was stunned into complete silence, which has never happened … in my entire life. And, I don't know if you know this, but I'm sure that I'm much older than you."

He pauses and I move my mouse to wake up my laptop and take a quick look at my email for no reason except to busy my hands and my mind because I'm terrified that I may pass out. Or worse, I will try to reply, but nothing will come out except a stupid sound because it's not even possible to form the right words.

I guess he's a mind reader in addition to believing in past lives because he says, "You don't have to respond. I just felt strongly that you should know what I was feeling and thinking." Then he turns and looks me directly in the eyes, his eyes burning into mine, just like they were last night, "I think we both experienced something special just being in each other's presence." Or did he say that? I can't be sure. It feels like something he might say but I'm so unstable right now that I can't be sure.

He notices that the presenter is now starting to speak, so he looks forward then back to me quickly and lowers his voice even further, "So, I don't know what this means for either of us, but I'm pretty certain that we were together in another life. What I have concluded after ruminating all night is that we probably traveled together in 16th century Ireland, mostly likely bringing joy and music to the masses. You did tell me that you are a musical marvel. Well, I have no doubt and I'm honored that I was your groupie."

He's married? He believes in past lives? I'm equally disturbed by both.

I give an awkward laugh and then we quietly listen as someone gives a long presentation on marketing, making a compelling case to the group about the $5 million investment he needs to get things on track. There are nods all around the room, then Jonathan speaks up with a slight raise of the hand and his voice booming, "Mark, I really want to thank you for the focus you've given this business over the last nine months, but I need to be very clear here that, unlike the incubation of a child that takes the same amount of time that you've nurtured this business, we are not in fact, growing a human body, we are only trying to sell our products through partners who know our business and can be persuaded without millions of dollars in investment."

He stands when he realizes that, since he's in the back of the room, many can't see him and he walks slowly toward the front of the room, his voice growing louder, "So, I ask that you adjust your plan to accommodate a quarter of the budget you request and that you and your team take a creative approach to the business and your project plans."

When he reaches the front of the room, he puts a hand on Mark's shoulder, his voice softens and he looks out into the audience, "We all understand where you're coming from, but I think we can all agree that our business has been a very difficult beast to tame so we will all need to team up here to find the right focus and solution." He let's go of Mark, gives him a smile and then faces the group, "I challenge all of you to be tenacious. Please do me and Dave a favor here by speaking up with your ideas and stepping up to be part of a more grassroots marketing approach."

For the next 30 minutes there is lively conversation around the room, people standing up sharing their ideas. Some are ridiculous, in my humble and uneducated point of view, but others are pretty good and I'm again reminded that I don't belong here.

The people, the ideas, the pure knowledge of numbers and business acumen are way out of my league. But I hang in there, being fed quick glances from Jonathan across the room. He has been seat-hopping all day. I now know that this is strategic, he's playing this room like a well-timed game of chess. It's working. Over the course of the nine-hour day, he has persuaded the entire group to his way of thinking on nearly every issue. There was one that didn't go his way, but I could tell that he really didn't care either way. Almost like he had to put up a fight for good measure. He's smart, charismatic and these people genuinely respect him. Yes, there may be some fear that I'm sensing, but overall, he's the guy in charge and they like him. I like him, too.

When the day finally starts to wind down, an hour and a half later than outlined on the schedule, I'm starting to get anxious about making my flight. It's nearly 5:30 and I take off from JFK at 7:15.

I circulate around the room saying my goodbyes, brief explanations about getting back to the kids and nearly everyone I approach asks why I'm leaving so early. "Why don't you just stay the night and we'll have some drinks tonight?" multiple people ask.

Once out of the conference room I feel immediate relief, but complete exhaustion taking over me.

I feel a hand on my shoulder as I take a step toward the automatic door that will take me out to the street where I'll meet my cab. Electricity runs through the left side of my body like I was shocked and I know immediately who is holding my shoulder. I can feel him, sense his presence and it takes my breath away. He slowly drops his hand from my shoulder and it slides gently down my arm, his palm resting on my tricep.

He says, "Hey, why are you off so soon?" He looks stricken, sad, and I notice. He continues, "Well, I just wanted to say that it has been an honor meeting you."

I open my mouth to respond but he cuts me off with, "I'm not exactly sure what happened between us, but I know it was something — something extraordinary." Or did he? Maybe that was my imagination getting the best of me. Well, if he didn't say it, I know that's what he meant.

I keep my gaze steady, not sure if I should stand here forever or run out the door as fast as I can. Conflict at its best. I blink, my eyes stinging from the overexposure to the oddly bright sun that's pouring into the hotel's floor-to-ceiling lobby windows.

I open my mouth to respond again, but nothing comes out. Finally I squeak out, "Jonathan, it was such a pleasure to meet you. Strange ... but definitely a pleasure." I put my hand out to shake his, but he just looks at it and laughs before pulling me in for a hug. His arms wrap around my body tightly. I feel safe and warm and, at the same time, completely terrified because I know in my gut that this will not be our last embrace and that my life will never be the same.

Chapter 4

My body is back home, but my head is miles away as I go back to real life. I'm both elated at my little secret and mortified that my encounter in New York confirms that I'm a terrible person ... something I've been convincing myself of since I was 10 years old, walking around in a haze of fear and alternate reality.

My face would be smiling, my mouth saying all the right words, but my mind wasn't there. It was worlds away, stuck in a dark shadow plagued with morbid images of the worst possible circumstances.

I lived between these two worlds. My teenage physical world where I would go through the motions, even managing to be a good student, named sweetheart queen and falling in love for the first time. My parents would ask me questions and I would hear my replies. Short, cold. Were they true? Was I fine, just a little worried about a test that was coming up?

"Why aren't you eating?" my mom would often ask, noticeably worried as she saw that my clothes were hanging off my already small frame, my face sunken in. My eyes were bulging, wide open like I was shocked at what my eyes were seeing. But that wasn't the case. I was in shock that while my eyes were stuck in my physical world, they couldn't see nearly as vividly as the pictures that were playing over and over in my mind. My eyes were failing me. They were registering a safe, normal life while my brain was playing a reel that showed me as a monster stuck in this frail body.

Images of every member of my family, dead, would race through my mind. I would sometimes be hovering over a coffin, their eyes closed and their skin cold. Just like it was when I said goodbye to my grandfather just before I turned 13. I was old enough to understand, of course, so I said goodbye and cried a million tears as I tried to wrap my hormone-imbalanced teenaged mind around the first death I had ever experienced.

I was filled with anger as I met grandpa's siblings and their extended families. It was a large clan, eight kids from grandpa's immigrant father and his Irish American wife. His parents died young and the family went their separate ways. Although they all lived within a few hours across Illinois, they were the opposite of tight knit. But it seems like the death of a sibling and a party that involved alcohol somehow brought everyone together. Their faces were flushed and their cups were full of beer as they toasted my frail and anxious grandpa.

They told childhood stories of playing tricks on him and throwing him in the local pond when they knew he couldn't swim. They laughed and I could feel the terror that grandpa must have felt, so I cried harder and then, when I couldn't take any more of the cheer, I hid in the basement. There it felt safe. The smell was clean from my grandma's meticulous laundry regime, mixed with the must and humidity from the half-finished interiors that had been there for centuries. I looked around and was flooded with memories and emotion. The antique typewriter was on an even older wrought iron desk with a roller chair in front of it. The seat covered in red bandana material that my grandma recovered herself. Red was her favorite color because it was the color that looked best on her olive skin and dark black hair. Red lipstick and red beads made her look like a movie star. From as early as I could remember, I would sit here swirling 'round and 'round, banging on that typewriter. I would write stories, poems, anything and everything that came to my nervous mind.

My grandma would sit with me for hours, teaching me how to hold my hands on the delicate keys so I could "build some good typist skills." Grandma was a brilliant typist, was proud of my diligence and would always compliment my creative writing. It took me years to see this, but she was a writer herself. She wrote jokes. Her very own, handwritten on recipe cards and organized — one box for "clean" jokes and one for the "dirty" jokes. We weren't allowed to see the dirty jokes, so she kept the box on a high shelf in the corner of her kitchen behind her fiesta chinaware. She didn't know we knew this hiding place until we were much older and then she decided to lock them away.

She was funny and smart and ruled the house like the Queen of England as far as I was concerned. She wrote a beautiful poem for my grandpa when he retired from the Mobil gas company and printed the poem on elegant paper as a gift, along with a miniature version of my grandpa's gas truck that was handed on to his successor. She read it at his retirement party in the living room in front of about 25 of their closest friends and family. There were tears in everyone's eyes, even the men and, in this family, men didn't cry. I watched them as they tried to blink rapidly or rub their eyes to play it off like there was some dust in the air or an eyelash gone rogue. But it was obvious that everyone was moved, regardless of their gender. There were roars of laughter as she wrapped up her passage. To me, it sounded like music and hearing the words burst from the mouth of my greatest role model sealed the deal for me. I wanted to be just like her. More than that, I wanted to live out my life doing all the things that she wanted to do, but never did.

She never spoke of her dreams out loud, she was content with the secure life she had built for her family. She was surrounded by adoring friends, always. But I could see in her eyes that she wanted to expand her boundaries, push the limits and, in my eyes, she was the yard stick I was measuring myself against.

After my grandpa died, the fear of losing grandma sent my brain and spirit on a downward spiral into the darkness. I told no one. Silently slipping away more and more each day into a kaleidoscope of horror fantasy. It felt dark, twisted, but it seemed that going there was easier than participating in my physical body. Facing the real fears in my life — losing my beloved grandmother and not living up to the crazy expectations I held for myself was much harder.

There were other fears, too. It felt like my family was living on the edge of destruction. My mom and dad worked hard and valued love above all else, but life wasn't easy for us — not financially, not emotionally, not in any way. It felt heavy and I felt like I was responsible. The voices in my head told me so. Maybe it was a birth order thing. Technically, Jamie and I are exactly the same age, but I took on the "first born" role with gusto. We do have an older brother, but he wasn't in the house, so I took his spot, too. When my younger sister and brother were born, I didn't have the jealous sibling thing. I was seven years old and I vividly remember thinking that I was responsible for these beings, that I needed to protect them above all else. At school, I would worry about them, make lists of ways to help them have more structure in their routine and add to the running list in my head of all the bad things that could happen to them. In my young mind, the world was a scary place — a world to navigate with extreme care and timid moves.

So I escaped. Day after day, challenging my brain to the deepest darkest valleys of thoughts that would take over all of me. So preoccupied that I was unable to eat, barely drink. Bringing myself to the brink of starvation, pushing my body to the limits. A very discreet way to slowly slip away from the present and live in the uncomfortable and satisfyingly self-destroying alternate reality. This became my reprieve in life. I would go in and out of this nightmare during times of stress. I told no one. Not even Jamie and we shared everything. I would say, "I'm not doing well, just feeling stressed." I couldn't bring myself to let her know what a terrible person I was. Even if I wanted to tell her, I had no idea what to say because I had no idea what was happening to me.

So here I am back at my home and I feel like for the first time in a long time, I may be on the brink of really living again. I don't know what that means, but it feels like there is a spark of light and it feels familiar. It reminds me of the me I was getting to know in my early twenties. Although I was still living in my sphere of fear, I was also learning to quiet it and I noticed that, when I took little leaps of faith, the dark thoughts would lessen. Like when I quit my job at 23 to go to New York on a whim (maybe that's an example of a "not so little" leap). I floated around the city with Lisa, my first college friend. Jamie and I met her the first day we were dropped off at Lawson Hall at Eastern Illinois University. "Harvard of the Midwest" students would joke. An affordable state school, it was a dream come true for me and Jamie. We were the first in our extended family to go to college and we vowed to take it seriously, make the most of it. Boy, did we. We worked at least two jobs each throughout our four years, got good grades and still found the energy to have the time of our lives. To this day, our closest friends crossed our paths on the EIU campus and are still the people I call in the middle of the night when I need an ear and some validation.

As Lisa showed me around her city, I fell in love with New York. The energy, the possibilities, the massive number of people. Maybe it's because I grew up in such a small town or that I'm an extrovert, but I longed for city life, felt invigorated by the buzz.

I spent three weeks hanging out, interviewing for jobs and dreaming about my life as a New Yorker. When I couldn't put it off any longer, I flew back to Chicago to tie up loose ends and plan my move. But life served up another route for me.

"Fitz," he screamed into my ear when I picked up the phone.

His signature move. Before caller ID, I always knew it was him; He was the only one that called me Fitz. Even after I got married he still called me by the shortened version of my maiden name. Rob had just moved from Chicago to Denver for work and I was sure he was calling to tell me that he was moving back.

"How was New York?" he asked, but didn't pause to hear my answer. Instead he jumped right to it.

"You have to come to Denver, you'll love it!"

Since I was embracing the free spirit side of myself, I did. I flew there the following week and, while I didn't covet the buzz of Denver as much as I did New York, I had to admit that the city had a good vibe, was much more realistic financially and, on the last day of my trip, he introduced me to my now husband. Long story short, I moved to Denver a few months after and was married a year later.

It's 10:30pm and I'm home alone with the kids. Our daily life is a bit like Groundhog Day, but the repetition felt sweet. The nighttime routines, reading bedtime stories, checking them multiple times in the night to be sure their breathing was regular. My hand on her back waiting frantically to feel it move up and down with her innocent breath.

I give myself strict deadlines. After I'm sure they're sleeping, I take a little time for a late-night snack of popcorn and Sprite; and sometimes a square of dark chocolate with caramel that dripped out when I pulled it apart. I set up my laptop in my bed and my work begins again by 8:15pm at the latest. I work on writing website copy or collateral until 11:30 or sometimes into the wee hours of the morning if I'm on a roll.

Up at 6:30 to help pick out school clothes, pack lunches and walk them across the street to school where I hug them goodbye and send them off with wishes like, "God bless you, you are perfect just as you are, spread joy to the world today."

I'm tired, oh so tired. But I'm happily distracted by the reel of last week's business meeting running through my mind over and over again. I am working on projects with Jonathan and there's nothing awkward about our working relationship. It's easy, productive, fun. Neither of us has mentioned our encounter as we build what I think is a solid friendship over work emails and conference calls.

I'm desperately trying to figure out what happened, dissect every word, straining my mind to read between the lines.

Chapter 5

"I will take the house and the kids," he's screaming at me. There's venom in his voice even though the volume is low. We're having this "discussion" in the closet of our master bedroom while the kids play in the basement. We don't want them to hear.

I want to scoop up my kids, take them to my mom's house and have her meet us at the door hugging me, but she's 800 miles away. I need my mom.

"Do you love him?" the question hangs in the air like dark clouds threatening a downpour.

I look down at my red toenails, freshly pedicured for my return trip to New York the week before. The work trip that I'm regretting. I was there to coordinate an event for the client's executives and sales managers. There was a hefty budget and I enjoyed spending it at one of the hottest clubs, renting out a private room, ordering fancy appetizers and coordinating the top shelf bar and DJ.

I bought a new dress for the occasion. Of course, I knew he would be there, but I wasn't prepared for what he said to me as we stood together near the DJ station where his colleague addressed the group, microphone in hand.

"Darling," he said and I looked at him like he was nuts. Did he really say that? Maybe not. Maybe he just said Amie and my emotionally starved self needs to be called a term of endearment.

"Darling, ha ha ha, yes, I think that in a past life I called you darling." Ha, I really did hear that right.

I took a big gulp of champagne and tried to hide the smile that was threatening to give me away. Giving away that I was completely flattered and loving the attention. But what the hell does he mean by past life?

He came closer, turning toward me and said in a whisper, "I know this is crazy, but it's true ... I think I love you."

What did he just say? That had to have been my imagination or maybe I'd had too much champagne. My ears were buzzing. Although I'm pretty sure that the party went on around us, to me, everything stopped. There were no more speeches, no buzz of conversation, no clanking of glasses or waitresses in low cut black dresses offering appetizers on silver platters. Everything stopped and all I could hear was my heart thudding under my form-fitting beige and black patterned boutique dress, my knee high black boots killing my feet, big toes throbbing.

I looked at him and he was grinning, a small laugh squeaked out and I relaxed.

"Yeah, I know what you mean," I whispered, looking him in the eyes.

I didn't know that I loved him, but I understood the sentiment. It made no sense. This was not good, but right then, I didn't really care. It felt right, felt good, felt like I was getting the appreciation and words of affirmation I was craving.

I was buzzed, not just on champagne and scallops, but on an emotional high that I hadn't experienced in over a decade.

The champagne flowed. There were VIP tables at clubs, dancing, hookahs and cigars. He was by my side as I danced around and met people from all over the world. One guy from Singapore came up to me as I danced alone in the middle of a cigar bar. I had met him the day before at the general conference, we exchanged information because he was also a contractor working for the Japanese business.

"Amie! I love your necklace. Where did you get it?" he asked, hugging me in a bear hug, typical for a midnight meeting on a pseudo dancefloor.

"My friend Caitlyn made it for me," I said in between lyrics of Rhianna's "We Fell in Love in a Hopeless Place." Like he had any idea who Caitlyn was, but the detail felt important.

"Nice. I am looking for something similar for my wife," he replied, then spinning me around.

I stopped spinning, undid the clasp of my necklace and handed it to him, then walked out of the bar, stumbling around looking for the bathroom. I was drunker than I'd realized. Must have been the hookah smoking.

I stumbled my way out of the bathroom stall and dried my hands without washing them. As I walked back down the long hallway toward the bar, I felt like someone was holding my hand, pulling me along in the opposite direction. I turn the other way and walk toward the elevators.

"Like I said, nothing happened between us, just an emotional connection that made me realize we are missing that. I think this means we need to work on us."

What do I know about love anyway? I don't know that I love anyone. Besides my children. That kind of love is immediate, unconditional and pure.

"Us? There is no us. When you decided to have an affair, us went out the window," his words spilling out angrily.

I told him about what happened that night right away. "Honesty is always the best policy," my mom and dad always told me. This seemed to be a situation where the truth would be the only way through. But it wasn't. The truth made me scared that I was about to lose everything I cared about.

He's sitting in his brown swivel office chair, it's pushed away from the wall where a hand-made desk shoots out. He built it when I started working from home. The office was my space since I spent so much time there on conference calls. Working with people all over the world, I would sneak down the stairs in the middle of the night or crawl out of bed at 5am a few times a week for my early starts with the Europeans. He travels every week so the tiny closet office is barely used, just to catch up on email or handle submitting travel expenses.

I'm split in two. The familiar part of me is crumpled into a ball, scared. How could I have messed my life up so badly? What kind of a monster am I to have hurt him so deeply? How could I have done this to my children? Why am I so evil? The barrage of questions shoot at me like a firing squad. This is a voice, but it's not that calm, loving voice I have been hearing lately. This one is harsh and it's impossible to quiet. Louder and louder it screams at me.

The other part of me is much smaller, but it is still. There is a knowing that I am not evil, that I am longing for something else, something more. Love. I want to be cherished. It feels like the essence of me. Not just the part about being loved, but all of it. Me being me. This guy certainly isn't the answer, but there is a secret desire that wants to awaken and it's bubbling to the surface. Through this crazy experience, it got a glimpse of daylight. I have a choice to make here in this closet. Do I let her fame rise or has she had her 15 minutes?

"By the way, I googled him. He looks like the typical slick business guy that has women all over. You were played, well done," he says as he walks out of the closet. I hear his footsteps marching down the stairs.

I consider following him, rationalizing with him. But I'm sure that he's right.

So I stay. Sitting in the same spot, looking up at our clothes hanging all around me. Mine on the right, his on the left, there is no overlap.

The shelves are piled with sweaters and old t-shirts. A handful of clear plastic bins stacked on the floor near where I sit. I bought them six months earlier, the result of a burst of organizing energy, inspired by a show on HGTV, of course. You know the ones where the designer goes in and makes all of the family's spaces functional and adorable. I wanted that. So I bought all new hangers so they matched, plastic bins and cute baskets that coordinated with the hangers. I did organize the hanging clothes, but that's as far as I got. On my side of the closet there are random gift bags and boxes that haven't been touched since we moved in five years earlier, labeled as memorabilia and paperwork. I have an uncontrollable urge to pull them all down.

So I do. Frantically. Taking my aggression out on the boxes as I toss them to the ground with a thud. One by one. I want to pull it all apart, dissect it and then put it back together again in a structure that I understand.

There is nothing clear in my head. Fear is clouding it all. I feel like a failure, a terrible person. How could I have allowed this to happen to my marriage? Is it possible that I will lose my kids, my husband and my home? What about my job? Nothing is certain. I feel like it's all mashed up; I'm not sure which one to worry about first. So I start organizing the closet. Going through box after box trying to make sense of anything. I put things in order with the hopes that my head will start to feel in order, too.

There's a Tiffany bag on the top shelf and it topples down onto my head when I reach for a plastic bin, which falls down right behind it. There are tears, but not because it hurt. I know this Tiffany bag. I saved it from my baby shower six years ago. Inside is a beautiful silver rattle, ribbons from a few of the gifts and a handwritten note from my mother-in-law. She is kind and loving and it reminds me of even more people I have let down. They have treated me like family and I love them. There are also rosary beads inside the bag and I am so grateful. Prayer and repentance is exactly what I need right now. I start to pray, but something catches my eye. It's my certification of baptism and confirmation from the Catholic Church. It's printed on beautiful thick gray speckled paper, it looks like a small diploma. I admire it and smile at the accomplishment. I was proud when my name was called at mass on a snowy Sunday morning. The name of my patron saint was also said aloud and I see her name here, too.

"St. Teresa of Avila"

St. Teresa of Avila. I say her name out loud and it feels good. There is peace and I suddenly don't feel alone in this closet, now a huge mess. All the things that were neatly tucked away are now pulled out into the open.

It's how I feel about my situation. Everything was fine. All my emotions and secret desires were packed away inside of me and safely guarded by my stubbornness, fear and doer mentality. I kept those needs at bay and anytime they would start to make a fuss, I quieted them down with a dose of shame and guilt.

"Oh really, you want to be appreciated and cherished? Well so does 'CinderAmie,' but she has work to do and she has a wicked stepmother to keep her in check. No such luck for you; ain't no fairy godmother going to bail you out, honey. This is your life and you should feel damn lucky to have it," my brain lectures me.

But here it is, it's all out and there's no going back. I could put it all back the way it was but that would have been a waste of time. I have no choice, but to go through it all, throw out the things that no longer serve me and keep the things that do. Then take the things that I decide to keep and restack them in a way that's practical and organized.

I work on this methodically for hours and, as I work my way through the last bin, my phone dings with a voice message.

It's him. "Are you ok? I got a call from your husband. You need to know I meant what I said and I want only the best for you."

I delete it and then hit "block caller." And put my phone down. I decide not to finish going through the last bin. I put everything back the way it was and I stick it up on the highest shelf in the corner, relieved that I don't have to look at anything else. Ever. Again.

(four years later)

Chapter 6

The house is quiet. Eerily quiet, even from my point of view. And it looks like children live here, but there isn't a peep of laughter and absolutely no commotion — I could hear a pin drop as they would say. If I had the ability to go back to the basic senses.

But I know they live here, I can feel it, plus I see photos of them hanging on nearly every wall in this very tidy home.

Two little girls. Oh, they are beautiful. I'm a little startled by the familiarity I see through their eyes in the photo next to the door — an image of the two of them wearing matching polka dot dresses and holding hands.

One, she looks like the oldest, has golden hair and bright blue eyes. Her soul has been in this world many times. The other, the younger girl, looks very similar in age, just a bit smaller. Her hair a dark brown with a hint of red with matching sparkly eyes. She too has been in this world many times and I know that the two of them have a big purpose in this physical world. I feel a flash of their stories and I know.

But I'm still interested. These photos give me a good view of the picture that's being painted right here and now at this suburban home.

Once you come into the blue door, situated just to the right of a wrap-around porch with white rocking chairs and a mountain view, I'm drawn to the wall above the staircase which is covered in black wooden frames. All shapes and sizes but they're hung perfectly in a way that's meant to look unintentional. More pictures of the two girls as I scan the light gray wall — from birth to what looks like elementary school age.

There are family photos, too. The girls with their mother and father in places all over the world it seems. I see them standing in front of the Eiffel Tower, hiking in Switzerland, buckled up on a roller coaster at Disney World. And a few photos of them standing on beaches and mountaintops; all different but with the same feeling of adventure.

It looks like they are having so much fun, really living life to the fullest. But I see another story.

I stop to take a closer look at the largest image on the wall. A black and white shot of the family of four. Here, I can really see their faces. The girls look young here, two and three years of age I'm guessing. Both look as if they have been caught in the middle of a laugh, likely a professional on the other side of the camera saying silly things for a reaction. Dad, on the left, has the same light eyes as the oldest daughter and looks amused. His teeth aren't visible, instead his lips are pushed together tightly with a hint of a smile starting to form. It looks unfinished.

Then, there's mom on the far right, with her head very close to the youngest daughter. They look so much alike with their dark hair and matching eyes. Her smile is wide, so big that I think I may see every tooth in her mouth and her eyes squinted. Her face looks drawn, her eyes hallow, but I see joy bubbling under the surface there.

I'm satisfied with what I've seen. But before I leave I go out to the porch and pull out a white rocking chair. I sit.

The chair doesn't recognize me so it doesn't move. I take a second to purpose my energy, then the chair gently rocks back and forth on the slate gray wood planks. In a second, I'm fully aware that this chair has never been used.

No one has ever sat here admiring the mountains lining the sunset in the distance. No one has ever rocked back and forth with a cup of tea. There have been no conversations or connections made on this porch between souls. It is empty. Now I know why I'm here. But I sit and rock a little while longer.

creeeeeeak

I wake up abruptly with a shutter, then sit up, looking around the room trying to figure out why I'm breathing heavily and my heart's racing.

Creeeeeeak … creeeeeeak

I hear from the front of the house. A rocking back and forth on the wooden planks. I look out the oversized windows to my right that look out over our backyard. From my usual spot in the middle of the bed I can see the tops of the young, Aspen trees peeking just above the window sill.

The tiny yellow leaves are perfectly still and I don't hear the gusts of wind that we've become accustomed to when we moved from Denver to Arvada. Just 15 miles northwest of the city, it's officially a suburb, but I've heard many of the suburban parents describing the town as, "unofficially the foothills."

One, because it made them feel better about their reluctant suburban status that they always swore off.

And two, because their healthy egos get a boost when bragging about their closer proximity to the mountains as compared to other Denver suburbs. In my opinion, suburbs are suburbs. It's pretty black and white and I'm not even the "black and white" type.

If I had to describe myself and my beliefs, it would be a wide-ranged gray scale. From the darkest of dark blacks to the hundreds of varieties of white — linens, snow whites and creams. And every single shade of gray in between. But on this topic I was quite clear. If you live outside the city limits of a major metropolitan city, then you have to take accountability, you are squarely in suburban territory.

We sold the cute little picket-fence house in the most desirable neighborhood in Denver when I was just weeks away from giving birth to baby number two. I cried as I packed up the 900 square-feet, 100-year-old home that meant the world to me. The one where

I envisioned we would raise our two young daughters, sending them to public school and walking the city streets as they learned to walk.

I sobbed as the realtor handed the keys over to the new owners, a young couple, fresh from New York. A big move to Colorado for the "mountains, quality of life and fresh air," they said when I asked them with alarm why they would ever leave the greatest city on earth.

Thoughts came rushing into my mind like a tidal wave; I see myself waddling out in the middle of the night, my big belly slowing me down, yet I'm nearly invisible in my all black maternity pants and giant sweater. I can see myself standing near the quiet, tree-lined street, calmly waiting for the moving truck that I have ordered to arrive in the middle of the night. Me and the two moving guys, I'll call them Al and Jim because those names sound appropriate for strong moving guys, but they are also loveable; they're quietly removing all of our furniture and poorly packed boxes from the Arvada-bound truck and slowly yet efficiently loading them into a New York-bound 18-wheeler. I have no idea if we have enough stuff to warrant an 18-wheeler but I figure, dream big or go home. I'm admiring the truck with "NY or Bust" in bright red letters across the back of it when a terrifying thought crosses my mind. No, it is more than a thought, more like a feeling that fills every cell of my body. Like a telepathic whisper that sends a shiver up my spine, radiating through me, head to toe ...

"Amie, you are not living your life."
"Live the life you are meant to live."

The words that aren't really words keep running through me like a broken record. Over and over again until my ears are ringing.

I am losing my mind, I thought. But before I can let the thoughts sink in and even consider taking action, I'm pulled back to reality when Evelyn face plants into a glass coffee table. I haven't even had the pleasure of climbing into the rig to drive across country before I'm running across the room, picking her up and consoling her. In 30 seconds flat, she's off again, no memory of a near-brain-injury.

I smile as she walks around with that drunk toddler, confident kind of swagger and my stomach catches. You know that feeling? It's not quite like the stomach flip that happens on a roller coaster. Much more subtle physically, but a thousand times more alarming emotionally. Kind of like being punched in the gut when you're least expecting it. And I've had this happen. A story for another time, but I will say that it was quite alarming and it knocked me sober.

This is not the first time my body and imagination have kicked into overdrive when it's too late. It's always during these 'pivotal' moments in my life when my body decides to fight against me. Some people describe it as butterflies or a "gut feeling." To me, it feels like there is a watered down version of me deep inside that's too frail and weak to speak up with advance warning.

Like I have a very lightweight super model inside me that refuses to live up to her fierce, diva-like potential. Now, I know that I'm not a supermodel. At 5'4" (and shrinking), with my build, bone structure and love for pizza, I'm fairly confident in my "never going to model for anything" status.

But for some reason, giving my higher self (or alter ego, if you will) a supermodel title feels right to me. I don't mean to be judge-y, but she fits the mold of frail and mute when it comes to giving me the signals I need.

Maybe it's because I've ignored her for so long? She's wasting away in my psyche, probably from neglect. She so badly wants to be the star, to stand out; be the center of attention. Although she's starved, she does get my attention every once in a while. And today this very lightweight supermodel keeps punching me in the gut. It doesn't hurt, but it startles me.

This little twist that feels like it's somewhere between my large intestines and my ovaries makes me think that these day dreams may have some validity. Either that or I have a stomach tumor, which I have noted to Google "stomach tumor symptoms" as soon as I leave here. But I am also nine months pregnant, so that could be a factor.

Why do I need to orchestrate an imaginary heist to get the city life that I want for me and my family? Why am I not doing it in waking life?

Why am I not screaming, "No, I don't want to move!" or "No, this is my life too and I get a say!" Or "I'm out of here and I'm taking my beautiful drunken toddler and nearly-baked newborn with me." Or "I want something different!"

Another gut tug, that tiny beautiful waif has just done it again and I can't quite figure out what to do. Do I say something, pull out of this because I know that I need to go another route? My head is spinning and I'm sweating, I can feel my chest flushing, heat rising up from my stomach all the way up to my throat. My throat is dry and I know that I'll be unable to speak these unspeakable words that are welling up. So I swallow them down. I say nothing.

So here I am, groggily waking up in my suburban home. It's quiet, minus the strange creaking noise from the front porch. It's always quiet, something I've grown used to since we moved here seven years ago. There is no picket fence or urban feel. Instead, a brand new home three times the size we need and a school across the street. I seem to have gladly traded in my longing for city life for a life that feels safe for my girls, now ages eight and seven.

We walk to school each day and we know all the neighbors. It feels more like a small town than a suburb. Jamie now lives just down the street and my closest friends are all in this neighborhood. We have playdates and babysit each other's kids. There is a sisterhood here that I'm deeply grateful for.

But I'm tired. Oh so tired. It's a Saturday and I have no idea what time it is, so I grab my cell phone from the nightstand that's way too low next to the silver Ikea bed frame that's piled too high with a giant box spring and plush mattress. It's the second mattress this year because I keep waking in the night drenched in sweat. It's like sleeping on a slip and slide. It's become a regular routine to wake up shaking with cold and looking like a drowned rat, removing all my clothes, the sheets, the comforter. Even the waterproof mattress protector soaked all the way through.

But today's a good day. My pajamas are damp and the back of my hair matted down so I know I sweated, but I slept through it and I'm relieved. I feel rested for the first time in a long time. No wonder. I glance at my phone, it's 10:11AM. That can't be right. So I google it and I can't help but laugh at my recent searches:

- Cause of night sweats
- Do I have a brain tumor?
- How old is Beyoncé?
- What is normal range of thyroid blood work

I add one more: "What time is it in Denver?"

"10:12am" it says. Confirmed.

Like most nights, I was up multiple times. I vaguely remember crazy dreams, getting up at 1am, again at 3am and then at 6am when I heard stirring, my family getting ready for their day of skiing.

I walk down the stairs to hug the kids goodbye and to be sure they have everything they need. Epi-pen, check. Snacks, check. Water, check. We exchange a quick look and then he looks away, busy packing up the car.

Chapter 7

I slowly make my way back up the 23 steep stairs, passing by the collage of family pictures on my way up. I look at them every time I walk these stairs, which is at least 10 times per day. I smile at the girls' tiny baby faces and sometimes I cry when I see the family pictures of us on our many adventures. I don't know why, but they make me sad. This morning I take a second to glance to my right at the most recent photo of our family of four and I do have a little bit of a pang of something when I remember the tension that circulated behind the scenes of the shot that now hangs in a black wooden frame.

Although I walk by this photo approximately 100 times per day and I know that the image is bright and cheery, it feels empty and I just don't know what to do with that. I keep climbing up the remaining 12 stairs and I slip back into bed.

The stairs, straight up, covered in tan carpet that's starting to look worn, a path down the middle where the girls run up and down them to get their toys, where they walk up slowly at bedtime, procrastinating the nightly routine. The worn path where I would run up and down multiple times per day as I did the laundry, when I couldn't find the phone, when I heard the girls screams as they fought over a toy or when their shrieks sounded like someone was dying, but then when I go to the top of the stairs where they were playing I would find that all was well, just part of their overly dramatic fun with Barbies or their American Girl Dolls. Me, doubled over and out of breath as I see their eyes light up and they burst into laughter when they notice that I'm there to split up a fight. They thought it was hilarious and I couldn't help but laugh as I looked at their elaborate set up for their dolls ... houses built out of tissue boxes, a string hung across the room as a zip line for their doll friends. Nearly everything from their rooms strung out all over the 500 square foot loft. With just a couch and chair, the sparse space was now full to the maximum, a sea of bright pink, bean bag chairs, pillows and blankets piled up as forts.

I make my way to the kitchen, fill the kettle and turn the heat on high. While I wait, I slip on my worn Birkenstocks and walk to the mailbox. There's a package, postmarked from New York, but no return address. My stomach leaps, my breath catches and I slowly walk back to the house without opening it, even though I'm dying to rip into the brown paper wrapping, carefully addressed with a black sharpie. The handwriting is neutral, could be a male or a female. It's printed in all lower case letters.

The tea kettle is screaming so I run to the door, past the dining room with the blue "accent" wall that I hate, into the kitchen, dropping the package onto the black granite counter.

I pour the boiling water into my favorite "I heart NY" mug and watch the steam rise as curiosity rises in me. But I try to swallow it down as the steam evaporates and my English breakfast tea steeps. I close my eyes, take three deep breaths, just as my brilliant therapist Jane has taught me to do, and I reach for the package. I make a small rip through the corner. There is another layer of brown paper to tear through, then I find what smells and looks like a very old book. There is no title on the cover, just a deep red leather binding with a thin gold line along the crease and accentuating the corners. I pick it up and look at the spine ...

PRIDE
AND
PREJUDICE

JANE
AUSTEN

1984

The spine is ornamented with the same thin gold lines on the front and the back, with a vine of flowers etched along the spine. Gold twists and turns, petals and leaves elegantly dancing down the spine of this beautiful book.

There is no note so I start flipping through the pages, carefully as I'm afraid to damage this precious piece of literary art.

I find one but I know that this inscription was not meant for me

To J. Comyns Carr

In acknowledgment of all I owe to his friendship and adore these illustrations are gratefully inscribed

- Hugh Thomson

Then I turn the page and see that Hugh Thomson illustrated *this* book. His name just two lines down from the famous name of Jane Austen. Typeset in a beautiful calligraphy serif font with a gorgeous illustration of a peacock poking his beautifully adorned head in between the illustrator's first and last names.

I can feel the significance of this important piece of literature, smell the layers of dust that have settled on this antique spine, nearly feel the nervous energy of the man who carefully penned his sincere words on the yellowing page of this book. I know it's from him even without a note or his name written in the blank spot that should have included the return address. He is here, I can feel his presence, like he's watching me, waiting for me to react. Hoping tears will run down my face and I will run to grab my phone to call him to profess my love, knowing that this book was a last ditch effort to get me to cave.

My sentimental heart beats fast and, although there are no tears left to be cried, I do agree that this would be a very profound time to shed a few superficial tears. Why not. If I'm going to play in the field of dreams, I may as well make it sappy.

But I don't cry. Instead, I am shocked when I find myself hurling the book across the room where its momentum is stopped by the espresso IKEA bookshelf that covers the north wall of my living room. It hits the corner, the glass candle holders and vases, that are strategically placed in the cubbies of the unit, shake and I hold my breath waiting for disaster to be followed by regret, but I'm relieved when the book just falls to the floor with a thud. There is no broken glass, no damage done. Relieved, yes, but shaken, and then I feel the flood gates open. With a sob, the tears finally start to fall and I'm a little bit satisfied that I could live up to this tragically romantic moment. The subject of my desire nowhere to be found. In fact, he didn't even bother to write down his return address or leave a note.

I rip up the packaging and bring it out to the dumpster so there's no evidence. I walk back up the stairs, one by one, ignoring the smiling faces to my right this time around. Too ashamed to look. I walk into the master bedroom and then to the left into the walk-in closet. It's way too big for the small amount of clothing and shoes that we have combined. "What a waste of space" I think as I climb up on the step ladder I keep nearby and I wrap the book in an old U2 concert t-shirt. It makes me smile. It was a gift from my friend Gina when we graduated college. We were 21 and our dramatic young adult brains were so unsure if we would ever see each other again. So as a token of our friendship, she gave me her favorite U2 shirt. Now *that's* friendship. Little did she know that we would still be friends, actually better friends than ever, as the years went by.

Now at 39, we talk every week and visit whenever we can. She has two kids of her own and lives in Chicago.

I finish wrapping the book inside the perfectly worn shirt, now off-white and soft from two decades of wear and washing, and pile all the other t-shirts on top. I climb down slowly. My balance is not so great these days, even though I have been doing yoga for years. I used to be the star student in class. No adjustments needed for me. I haven't been to a class in more than two years. My joints too swollen, my muscles too weak and still no answers as to why.

I fold up the ladder and bring it downstairs — my insurance policy that no one will find it because no one in my house is tall enough to reach the top shelf.

Chapter 8

Recent Searches:

- Photos of John Kerry on a sailboat
- Best brand of mascara
- Chronic Fatigue Syndrome
- Recipes for vegan brownies

Three days later I receive a call from Dr. Foster's nurse, Jacquelyn.

Her voice matches the blond, bubbly young girl I met at his office. She'd chit-chatted with me as she took my vitals and very politely asked if I wanted to remove my shoes and heavy sweater before I got on the scales. Of course I did. What woman wants to leave on the layers when it comes to documenting her weight?

"Hi, is this Amie I'm speaking to?" she asks.

"Yes, it is, hello Jacquelyn, thank you for calling," I respond as I try to quietly, yet frantically, continue getting ready. I have an appointment with a new therapist. I must be an overachiever. This will be number three in my therapy dream team. Jane, our couple's therapist and now someone new. Her name is Mirielle, recommended by one of Jamie's closest friends, Jane. She's going through a divorce and says that Mirielle is helping her through meditative therapy. I have no idea what that means, but at this point I'll try anything.

I decide brushing my teeth would be too obvious, so I start applying my mascara instead. I'm leaning up against my marble counter trying to get as close to the mirror as possible without climbing on top of it. I crank my neck to the left, balancing the phone between my shoulder and cheek and try my best to cover my lashes with black and coat them well. I'm hoping that it will help me look more awake than I actually feel.

I'm working on my right eye when she delivers the news, "Dr. Foster asked me to call you to let you know that all of your bloodwork is within normal range. Your liver enzymes and potassium levels are a little raised, but nothing to be concerned about."

A tear falls from my right eye and I blink for a little too long. I feel like going back to sleep at this very moment. I should be relieved, happy that there is no bad news to report.

But I'm not. I'm shattered that my blood isn't telling the same story that my body is telling every day; that I can barely get out of bed. Or that there are days when I can barely send a text because my hands tingle and hurt with every small movement. Or the days at work when I spend an hour trying to remember a very basic word like *negotiate*. My work, my marriage and my life are suffering.

"I need an answer now, Jacquelyn!" I want to scream into the phone. But I don't.

Instead, I am quiet as she goes on, "Dr. Foster will call you later this week with next steps, but it is very good news that the serious conditions are ruled out."

"Well, could the high liver enzymes and potassium be indicators of something going on?"

"No," she says. "The levels are slightly raised, but not conclusive in any way. It could be an indicator that you're taking Tylenol or other pain medications," she assures me.

I guess that could be true, I think. I have been taking Advil more often lately.

"Thank you for calling with the great news," I say flatly as I hit "End" and more tears come rolling down my face, streaks of black mascara along with them.

I look up into the mirror and I don't recognize the person looking back at me. She's a shadow of the person I remember. The cheeks sunken, eyes red-rimmed and surrounded by bluish/blackish circles. I don't know her and I'm certain that I don't ever *want* to know her. What should have been elation that all is well inside is a reminder of what I already knew. If my blood and body are normal, there is no sign of disease, then it is me that is not normal.

That call ends up being the first of many with the same outcome, although my reactions start to become less dramatic each time.

I start getting used to the statement "within normal range" and take it for what it is, another form of rejection. Unfortunately, it feels harder to take than being rejected by another human being. It's my body rejecting me.

I have traveled all over to see the best endocrinologists, neurologists, rheumatologists, even a specialist in infectious disease. All in a last ditch effort to find a reason for my rapidly deteriorating health. If I could just fix it then my life will go back to normal.

My weight now dips down to 100 pounds and I'm too weak to exercise. I continue on, pushed a little harder and, although I was not working at the same level my boss and colleagues are used to, I was present. Well, as present as I could be and doing my best to hang on.

What was I hanging on to? I don't know. It felt like an invisible rope that seemed to follow me everywhere I went. It showed up for the kids and for my work every morning, a reminder that there was something to grasp onto. It was there on those days that I was too tired and in pain to go to work and stayed in my bed for hours on end, drifting in and out of sleep. Only crawling out of bed to pee and to go to the kitchen for food and to refill my water glass.

My husband is here; he checks on me and tells me that things will get better, that we will find answers and will fix it. He started sleeping in the guest room so that he wouldn't further disrupt my sleep. I was grateful, but lonely. So very lonely in that bed.

But that invisible rope was there. Whatever it was, it comforted me and gave me a strange feeling that everything would be OK. I'm not religious and you would never catch me talking about God, but the only way I can describe the "invisible rope" is that it felt spiritual in some way. Maybe I was hallucinating, but maybe not.

Finally, Dr. Foster suggested that I come back in for a follow-up to check in on my prognosis. This is where he broke the news, "Amie (still that little French thing he did with the 'Ila'), you have seen a number of the best specialists in the country and all of your testing has come back normal; which we're very grateful for."

"Yes, very grateful," I lied and couldn't fight back tears.

"I understand that you're still not feeling well and that you're losing weight. Now, I want to be clear that your weight is not a concern for me, you are a very thin woman, but your BMI is still within a healthy range, so please do not let that be a source of worry for you."

He looked at me tenderly, sensing my uncertainty. My husband was there, so he turned to him and it reminded me again of John Kerry. Just like a politician delivering a speech, he was looking around the room to make connections with his audience.

He continued, "I have done a little research on your case, as it's unusual and one with very little to no evidence of a medical condition."

Husband nods in approval of Dr. Foster's assessment. He has told me hundreds of times that, after all this time and money, since there are still no answers, it's time to give up the hunt.

Then the doctor turns to me, "There is something called Chronic Fatigue Syndrome, which you have likely come across if you've been searching online for your own medical answers."

He pauses and I can tell that he knows that I have been frantically searching every disease from lymphoma to brain tumors, absolutely sure that I'll be able to identify something that fits my description and I can be done with this. Don't get me wrong, I do *not* want a brain tumor. But I do want an answer and I know with every fiber of my being that this answer will free me from the hell I'm living.

He laughs at his statement like it was a little joke and goes on, "We call this a syndrome because it is a set of medical signs and symptoms that are correlated, but we don't have enough evidence to call this a health condition or disease. What you're experiencing can't be explained by an underlying medical condition. We don't know much about the genesis of CFS, but we do know that there is a psychological component here that we can definitely treat," he explains. "I would like to put you on a low dose antidepressant. I think that will help get things under control for you."

He went on with his instructions, even as I felt like I was going to vomit all over his very beautiful antique desk, "Now, you can continue to take the nerve pain prescription you received from your rheumatologist. Has that been helping with the pain in your wrists and ankles?"

"Yes," I lied (again). He liked that answer, so he wrapped up our consultation and sent us on our way.

Maybe this is my life now. A life of sickness and searching for answers to fix me. I have tried it all. So I add the antidepressant to my cocktail of pills and supplements. So many that I have an oversized daily pill sorter. It's bigger than my laptop and surely meant for someone 80. All I can think about right now is brownies. I need to drown my sickness and my sorrows in a nice batch of brownies.

Chapter 9

Recent Searches:

- Is Real Housewives of New York scripted?
- Kidney stones
- How many people die each year under anesthesia?
- How do you know if your problem is your health, job or marriage?
- Alien abductions

I'm watching "Real Housewives of New York." It's past midnight. The sound of middle-aged women yelling at each other is surprisingly relaxing and I find that their drama puts my life's circumstances into perspective quite nicely. It's become my guilty pleasure since I've been recovering from surgery. To me, "surgery" sounds a little too serious for this event. I was under anesthesia and back home all in the same day. But even though the turnaround was quick, it certainly wasn't painless and my pain is physical, emotional and spiritual. Pain around the horn. "Around the horn," a phrase I learned in my many years of playing softball. So for those reading who are not versed in softball lingo, it means throwing the ball around the infield before it goes back to the pitcher. Kind of like a show of celebration after an out.

The week before, I was at the soccer field, standing with my soccer mom friends. Some who take soccer very seriously and some who like to chit chat like me and struggle to just get the kids there on time and in the right uniform.

"I won't be here next week," I say to the three beautiful ladies standing to my left and right. We're in a small circle catching up on the latest gossip, soccer complaints and usual mom banter.

"Why?" asks Gwen. She's *the* soccer mom of the group. She plans all the tournaments, even purchased customized shirts for the girls so they could look cute for their summer league. Her eyes widen like a light bulb has just gone off and she cuts me off as I start to answer ...

"Oh, Amie. I'm so excited for you that you're getting your boobs done," she says, dead serious.

She goes on, "I fully support your decision, Amie"

She's honest and sincere and I'm truly touched, but I can't get a reply out because I'm trying to form a sentence, but can't because it's so hilarious that she's assuming that I'm getting implants just because I mentioned surgery. Granted, I'm an athletic 32A so, yes, it's pretty obvious that I am a candidate for the procedure, but I have never considered breast enhancement. Never.

Not even when I went to Nordstrom for a proper fitting and they only had one bra in their inventory that was small enough for my non-existent bosom. This was a few years ago and I was excited to go experience the impeccable Nordstrom customer service.

"Hi. I would like a bra fitting, please," I said to the young woman behind the desk. Her hair like black silk and her makeup perfect. She looks like she could be part of the Kardashian family. She asks me to wait while she finds the right attendant to help me out and off I go to the dressing room where I'm expertly measured and I discuss my bra wish list.

"I could use something strapless and probably one or two bras in black and nude in order to keep it neutral and functional," I say as she wraps the measuring tape around the widest part of my rib cage.

I put my shirt back on while I wait for her to come back with my options. I'm grateful to be here and feel like I've made it. Years ago, I watched an "Oprah" episode where she interviewed doctors about women's back issues.

"Could your bra be to blame?" the teaser kept running and I was intrigued, especially since I had been wearing a nursing sports bra for two years. I had two of them and I would just rotate — white one day, black the next and so on. It was easy, comfortable and definitely practical. Even when I wasn't nursing, I continued to wear them. I didn't need the easy flap to expose my nipple anymore, but it wasn't a big deal. It just stayed snapped tightly. No use wasting a good bra and the $40 I had invested. Oprah and her bra expert recommended that all women go to Nordstrom for a free and expert fitting to save them from painful back pain.

I was expecting her to come back with an armful of bras to try on and I'm a little deflated when she shows up with one bra. One. So the visit didn't take long. I bought the one bra in the Nordstrom inventory that fit and I was on my way.

"Oh, vaginal rejuvenation!" Gwen yelled, excitedly. "I would totally do that, too. Good for you!" The other two women in our little circle are looking at her and then me, anticipation on their faces.

"Gwen, Gwen, settle down," Constance jumps in when she sees that I'm laughing too hard to reply. So she replies for me, "Amie's having a kidney stone surgically removed."

The faces around the circle change drastically, from amusement to disgust. I'm pretty disgusted myself. Three weeks ago, a stabbing pain on my right side woke me up in the middle of the night. I couldn't walk and was convinced that my appendix had burst so my in-laws came to the house, one staying with the kids and the other driving me to the emergency room where I went through a battery of tests while I was in and out of excruciating pain.

"Kidney stones," declared the young doctor who looked a lot like my little brother. Skinny, reddish hair and glasses that I think he wore only to make him look older.

"What?! Are you sure?" I ask, confused and drowsy from the pain meds being pumped into my IV. How could this be? I have chronic fatigue whatever and, since my last visit with Dr. Foster, I've seen a handful of other specialists. Lyme disease, Reactive Hypoglycemia, Addison's disease, even migraines have all been thrown into the diagnosis pot. It's all swirling around, taking on the other flavors. Kidney stones is not a welcome ingredient.

"Yes, quite sure," he says, not missing a beat, like he has answered this question many times before. Likely because everyone else, like me, is disappointed that their pain is wasted on a diagnosis as silly as kidney stones. Appendicitis, ruptured something, or an ovarian cyst, sure! Those I could get behind, and I'd be able to justify the pain I had just encountered. But stones in my kidney? This is ridiculous and I'm pretty sure I don't believe him even though he has reassured me by pointing out the CT scan report.

He writes me a prescription for Flomax, a drug that was developed for old men with prostate trouble so they can pee more freely. He says, "It works to help pass the kidney stones, helps expand the ureter so the stones can pass more easily."

My eyes bulge when he tells me that I will have to try to pass the stone on my own. Imagine a giant rock passing through a passage the size of pencil lead and there you go, you now have a visual of kidney stone logistics.

He gives me the name and number of a urologist and tells me to call him within a week if I haven't passed the stone. I leave with a wounded ego and a strainer to pee in so I can catch the slippery little sucker. If you are awakened in the middle of the night with stabbing pain and have to call your in-laws for help, the least he could do was help me walk away with a diagnosis more substantial than "kidney stone." It's embarrassing.

I don't pass the kidney stone over the next week, even though I'm putting all my hopes and energy on doing so, and I pee diligently into the strainer that rests under the toilet seat.

Dr. Hassan's waiting room is filled with old men. I'm the youngest by 20 years and the only female in the room, besides the overly-friendly receptionist. She walked me to the bathroom and I was concerned that she was going to stay to help me take the urine sample.

He walks in and my breath catches. Literally, I gasped. He looks like Aladdin, or what I would imagine Aladdin looks like in real life instead of being a cartoon. His skin creamy tan, his hair thick and black. About six foot tall and dressed like, well, a doctor. But more like a doctor at a night club because he's stylish and he smells good. Oh no, I forgot why I'm here.

"Dr. Hassan. Nice to meet you," he reaches to shake my hand.

"Nice to meet you, I'm Amie," I reply, my face burning with heat. I'm sure my cheeks and chest are bright red and giving me away.

"So, looks like you ended up in the ER over the weekend," he says to his laptop, where I assume he's looking at my file.

I don't respond because I'm pretty sure it's a rhetorical question, so I just sit on the exam table, the white paper crackling with the slightest shift of my body.

"That's a pretty good sized stone in your left ureter," he grimaces, concern in his voice.

He examines me and, I'm not going to lie, I sucked in my stomach and tightened my abs as he poked around my abdomen. It did hurt when he touched the left side, but I lied when he pressed down hard and looked at me for a reaction, "Not pain really, just tender." He smiled a very gentle you're-pathetic-and-I-don't-believe-you kind of smile.

I'm sure all the young women with kidney stones had a similar reaction. He's probably used to this. The humble life of a hot urologist. When he told me that Jane would be in to see me in a few minutes to schedule surgery I was stunned. Surgery for a kidney stone? Yes, I was in and out of significant pain, but this seems ridiculous.

He was giving me 10 more days to pass it on my own, otherwise he would see me in the operating room.

I spend the next 10 days chugging water, squeezing lemons and even went back to yoga, convinced that some difficult poses might prod it out. I strained my urine and was disappointed every time I didn't find a tiny pebble. Sometimes I was fine. Other times, I couldn't even walk. Climbing the steep stairs to my bedroom each night was exhausting and it took me an embarrassingly long time to hoof it up them. I would cramp half way up. I would take each step slowly and look to my right as I would go, noticing the family pictures that hung there. The pictures of my girls made me smile. I could step back into that exact time, know the stage of life that they were in. But the family pictures still made me feel uneasy.

Something was off. I transported myself to that mountain in the Swiss Alps, where we stood as a family of four, majestic mountains and pastures of green, a backdrop that looked like we were standing on the set of "The Sound of Music." I put myself in that backdrop, behind that tilted smile. My anxiety was high, my body was depleted and, while I was grateful to be part of this spectacular scenery, I didn't want to be there at all. I felt placed there rather than part of it.

So every night for 10 nights I looked at this photo and it brought up some serious emotions that I doubt I've ever examined. Tears would flow as I hiked up to my room where the dark soul of night awaited me. I was alone, my husband either traveling for work or sleeping in the basement so he wouldn't disturb my sleep. The questions swirling in my mind as I willed it to shut up and go to sleep ...

"Maybe I'm questioning because I'm sick and in such pain?"
"Maybe I'm just not a travel person?"
"Maybe I'm just not happy in my marriage?"
"Maybe I'm just too stressed with work?"
Or maybe it's all of the above.

The day of surgery finally arrived and I was feeling a mixture of fear and relief. But I was convinced that I had somehow already passed it and Dr. Hassan would get into my ureter and find nothing.

What a waste of time and energy, I thought, as I took deep breaths when the very nice nurse, named Angel, felt around for a juicy vein to insert my IV.

She held my hand, helped me through some long, deep breaths and reassured me that the anesthesia would not kill me. And, "Yes, Dr. Hassan has done this procedure thousands of times and you'll be just fine."

I'm aware that I sound like a big baby going through such anxiety over a quick procedure that doesn't even involve a scalpel. I'm not proud of my reaction, but at least I'm being honest and sincere. That has to count for something.

"Speak of the devil, here he is now," she says with warmth and I find it ironic that her name is Angel and she used an expression about the devil.

"Amie, here we are," he says, his smile cuter than I remember, reaching to shake my hand.

I jump in immediately, "Yes, so, I don't think I passed the stone, but I can't be sure. I just have a feeling that I may have passed it and didn't catch it. I'm really not feeling any pain, just a little cramping, which could mean that I did pass it and I'm healing from it."

I take a deep breath because I was talking very fast and holding my breath with my dissertation. A very weak attempt at hoping to be told that the surgery is cancelled and I can have my IV removed and be on my way.

"Ha, ha, ha," he laughs at me.

"Amie, I know that you don't want this surgery, but I'm certain that the stone is still there and, if it's not, I won't charge you for the procedure," he winks and then looks over my shoulder and introduces himself to my husband.

I can see that he's signing paperwork and checking off boxes, asks me to sign the consent form and I can feel that this surgery is only moments away. Panic rises and I give it one last effort.

"If I have to go back to the operating room, I would like to wear my glasses so I can see. The nurse told me I have to take my contacts out, but I can't see anything at all. Plus, I'm really worried that you're going to go in there and accidentally go into the wrong side. How do you know what side the stone is on?"

I have more to say on this topic, but he cuts me off.

"No problem, you can wear your glasses. I'll veto Angel on that one if it makes you feel better."

There's a long pause before he continues,

"As for going into the correct side — this isn't my first rodeo. However, hmmmm," he says, pulling a Sharpie from his pocket. He walks over to my bed, pulls up my gown signs his initials on my left hip. A very loopy SH that tingles across my hip bone and then all the way down into my bare everything. I'm obviously wearing no underwear since that area will be the entry point of the laser that will remove the rock that's causing all this drama and pain in my life.

I'm stunned to silence and he smiles in victory. That shut me up and kept my mind pretty occupied as I went through the rest of the setup. I was drugged, wheeled back to the operating room where I had to get up off the wheelie bed and get on the operating table myself. The least they could do was put me on the operating table. I had to sit in a specific position and was instructed to relax as the anesthesiologist asked me questions and put God knows what in my IV. In order to relax, I kept repeating:

"For I am the Lord your God who takes hold of your right hand and says to you, do not fear; I will help you."

Is this a Bible verse? Sounded like one to me and I have no idea where it came from since I don't read the Bible, even in my days of church hopping and hanging with the Christian kids in high school. But it helped, so I said it over and over again. I was surprised I even knew a Bible verse, let alone one that actually made sense to me and brought in a flood of peace. I could feel my right hand being held. Maybe Angel was holding it or maybe it was God or maybe I was losing my mind. All of the above?

I was fully awake at this point, just waiting for the anesthesia to kick in, which I was pretty sure wouldn't work on me. My mind was convinced that I would wake up in the middle of the procedure screaming for my life. I waited. Then I felt that deep whisper that filled every cell say very clearly, "Look up"

I jumped, looking around at the people in the room, busily moving instruments, looking at watches, taking instructions from each other. No one was looking at me or talking to me.

"Look up" I felt again, this time deeper, clearer. So I looked up and I was grateful that I requested my glasses. There He was, sitting in thin air just above all the operating commotion. Jesus. He was wearing a white robe and just felt like love and safety. He didn't speak with words, but with energy. "You will be ok. I am holding your right hand."

I felt my hand being squeezed and then I drifted off into the light.

When I woke up, I was talking and the nurses pushing me down the hall were laughing. I vaguely remember saying something about my excellent kickball skills because I felt like we were in the middle of a conversation about this, but when I saw their laughing faces I felt embarrassed, like I may have been the only one having this conversation at all. Dr. Hassan stopped by to say hello and show me the stone he retrieved while I slept. I was relieved that he got the correct side and that there was something for him to remove. Otherwise, I would have felt embarrassed and like I was wasting his time. I don't remember much of the conversation, but I do remember him saying that I would come back to his office in a week to have the stent removed. I had no idea what he meant by stent, but I was excited that I had a scheduled appointment to see him again.

I was a little buzzed as Jamie collected me from the recovery room and brought me home. She helped me up those damn steep stairs, me shuffling and her holding me up, her arms wrapped around my waist to keep me from failing. Then she deposited me on the right side of the bed. I vaguely remember waking up in the middle of the night to turn off the TV and take off my glasses. A ritual that I've grown accustomed to, which I know is not good for "quality sleep." But what happened next I'll never forget.

I was sleeping, like REM kind of sleep. Then there was a tap on my shoulder. I sit up fast. But I'm not scared, I'm happy, blissful. Whomever tapped me on the shoulder I'm excited to see or whatever it is I'm experiencing. But I don't *see* anyone or anything except the dark room and a billowing light hovering above the carpet near the foot of my bed. There's no one else in my bedroom to witness this. But I look around anyway, wishing I could say to someone, "Hey, wake up, do you see this?" I'm not sure why I'm surprised. I've been sleeping alone in this room for the past six months. I'm not dreaming, I'm completely lucid. I didn't drink last night and didn't even take an Advil, let alone an Ambien or something else that could be potential grounds for seeing crazy stuff like this.

I watch it circle around my bed, billowing playfully. The more it dances around, the happier I feel. I feel protected and safe. I don't know what it is, yet I know without a doubt that it is a spirit of some kind here to say "Hello" and "Wake up, wake up, wake up." "Don't worry, I've got you covered."

I am awake, really awake for what feels like the first time ever. It lasts maybe two minutes, but I can't be sure; I have no concept of time and this feels more important than time.

When the silky spirit disappears under my bed, I stick my head under to see if it might be hiding. There is nothing. It's gone and I'm grieving for it to come back. I grab my journal and pen from the nightstand and start taking notes as fast as I can. I don't want to forget this.

If it were aliens, there could be potential that they will wipe out my memory, so I better write it down so people will believe me. So that I — that *I* — will believe me.

Chapter 10

Recent Searches:

- Therapists near me
- Listing of autoimmune diseases
- If/Then musical lyrics
- How do you become a Broadway star?
- How to listen to signs from God

"So …" she said, letting the word hang there. "So," I say back, knowing what she wants to know, but not wanting to be so eager to talk about myself, again. For someone who is uncomfortable with talking about herself, I feel like I have been indulging in self-centered behavior for the past six months. My friends are now used to hearing about my life.

I've always been a good listener. But it seems that the tides have turned and here I am, dominating the conversation and talking about myself so much that I'm sick of me. I'm also aware that it's very ironic that I'm writing an entire book about me. I get it.

Granted, there were a lot of things "going on" in my life, but none of them interesting as far as I was concerned. But Mary sat there with her caring look and validating words, letting me talk and talk and talk.

"I just feel like I'm on the verge of a major change in my life," I say, sipping my Titos and soda with a lemon. And I feel egotistical talking all about me even though she is asking and listening intently. Responding at all the right times. She's so sincere and I know that she really wants to know; I feel safe telling her the real thoughts that keep me up at night.

"My work is crazy. My health keeps on declining and my marriage is in trouble," I whisper like I'm afraid that I'll hear it myself.

She nods and I can see that tears are welling up in her eyes.

"When every area of your life is falling to pieces, how do you know which to pick up and put back together again? Do I let them all fall and rebuild again?" I wonder out loud as Mary listens. She really listens, with eye contact and great concern.

"I have been picking up each piece carefully, looking at it, examining it, feeling the pain or joy or whatever emotion it brings and then putting it back down again. I feel scattered as I walk around each one, trying my best not to trip up or step on a sharp edge. But I know that I can't do this forever. It's exhausting, all this tip toeing," I say clearly and loudly and I know what I said is true.

This was news to me. I didn't realize I felt this until the words came out. Where did those words come from? Too definitive and graceful to be from me. It felt like another version of me, a higher, smarter, better me. Is she me, too? And if she is, where the hell has she been? Why doesn't she show up more often? Well, I like her and I hope she sticks around awhile.

"Amie, I'm so sorry you're going through this, but I know that you'll be OK. More than OK," she says with such compassion and love that I want to hug her and cry on her shoulder the rest of the night. But I know that's not possible because we have tickets to see a musical at 7:30.

"Keep listening to your gut. The universe has your back and will guide you in the direction you need to go," she says as we sign our credit card receipts.

I let that sink in as we walk to her brand new Audi. I'm jealous of how clean it is and make a mental note to take the kids with me to the car wash tomorrow. All three of us love a clean car.

"It's funny you should say that," I say as I buckle my seat belt. "I've had these weird things happening to me and I don't know what they mean. It's like I'm being watched or guided or something," I say in a small voice, afraid that she might think I'm crazy.

"Well, maybe it's the universe or God or angels shining some lights on things you need to notice," she's says like it's no big deal. "It doesn't matter what it is; I don't think we'll ever know, but it doesn't matter as long as you listen."

Her words sounds like the truth. We move on to talking about the kids, their school and activities as we drive the 30 minutes toward the Denver Performing Arts Center where we find out that our tickets are even better than I expected. Fifth row orchestra. OMG, I'll be able to see Idina Menzel's sweat. Maybe she'll spit on me while belting out a super high note.

The anticipation of sitting in a theater seat waiting for the lights to go out makes me feel like a child. What I would imagine childhood anticipation feels like. I have very few memories of my younger years. Really, I don't have much of a memory until I was in high school. There are fuzzy memories of being about 10, the anxiety, the worry, but that's it. I can't remember details or family jokes. Nothing. I thought this was normal until I got married and would sit with my newly-attained family and listen to my husband and his siblings share story after story from their youth. Detailed stories; dates, clothing worn, exact word spoken, that kind of thing. I didn't understand this and initially just chalked it up to their family genes being stronger with memory. I was never a great test taker, so thought it could also be a symptom of poor information retention I experienced.

I had an "Aha" moment when I went to my first therapy session. I was 33, the kids at home, ages 3 and 2, and I finally decided to look up a therapist online and go figure out some stuff. I was looking for a quick fix, someone to say, "Yes, you are anxious and this is why," and then they would list out all the reasons. I would take notes and write down the top three things I need to do and the book that I need to read in order to get it all sorted. She would also hand me a prescription that will help me take the edge off and, after a week or two, I would be back to my old self, walking around joyous and carefree. Like a sinus infection. Identify the problem, treat it, maybe take it easy for a few days but that's it. Zap it and move on.

I learned very quickly that the process doesn't work this way. It was quite disappointing.

I met Jane on a Friday in her tiny office in Louisville. She was just as pretty as her photo on the website. I found her photo as a search result for psychologists nearby, a listing from Psychology Today popped up and I scanned the list of therapists within a 10-mile radius. This is a little embarrassing, but I picked her because of her name. I liked the name Jane, and in the photo she looked like someone I could relate to. She looked kind and loving. I was right. Either I have a great instinct or I just got lucky. I'll never know. But I do know that she has become a fixture in my life and I've spent the last five years working with her through the toughest parts of my life.

She held me when I cried. Gave me the tough advice when I needed it, and listened. Oh boy, did she listen. I started to feel bad that I did so much talking so I would bring her an iced coffee from Starbucks. She probably didn't even drink coffee but of course, she drank it and was nothing but gracious, kind and wise. I love her and, to this day, I credit her for the woman I have finally become. I'm sure that she doubted her effectiveness and my ability to graduate from therapy as I watched my file grow larger and larger over the years.

At my last appointment, she said, "Whoa, it's getting heavy. I'm starting to wonder if I'm not doing my job," as she pulled out the file that was thicker than my water-logged mattress.

Of course, she was kidding and spent the next hour reassuring me that this was an attempt at humor rather than an accusation because she knows me so well. That I'll spend the next hour talking about the things she wants me to talk about, but thinking about my failure as a therapy patient who is unable to move on. I worry about her retirement. I even worry about the possibility of an untimely death. She is much too young to die of natural causes. Even considering that she may leave me makes my heart palpitate. I need her validation and advice. Otherwise, how will I function? My connection to her reminds me of the bond with my grandma. I can lean on her and the thought of her not being there and doing life without the sounding board makes me panicky.

She recommended a couples therapist, too. We went a few times, but it seemed to ignite our issues more. The best outcome of couple's therapy was a recommendation to a doctor for me at the end of our second, and final, visit; she handed me a sticky note with a phone number. "Call him, he's an expert at helping the un-diagnosable," she said after I handed her a check.

"The un-diagnosable," I thought. Saying it over and over again in my mind on our quiet drive home. Maybe that is who I am. The person who doesn't fit in a box. Maybe I'll never be normal again.

As I sit in the velvet seat just 100 feet from a Broadway star, my body feels like stone, still. Goosebumps crawl up my arms, my coarse hairs standing on end as I listen with my whole body to the lyrics coming from her miraculous voice straight to me.

"The marriage, the mortgage, I left them behind me before they could kill me?

My plan was perfect, courageous and daring, to start my life new.

Now I look at this morning, it moves me to say,

Oh my God, what did I do?

I can do this I know, I just need to take care

Be smart, self-sufficient, and hyper-aware

Cos I'm flirting with 40, there's no time to wait

And I can't help but feel I'm already too late ..."

I can't believe the lyrics. It literally sounds like she's singing directly to me, giving me the validation and direction I've been asking for. Mary notices it, too, she turns to me and mouths, "Oh.

My. God." And she just looks at me for a few seconds, her mouth wide open.

As she continues with the next chorus, "'Cos I'm flirting with 40 there's no time to wait ..." I am laughing and crying at the same time. I feel like God just sent me a message through a Broadway diva. Words of wisdom and motivation through a Broadway musical. Brilliant. Shocked; I hadn't thought that the Divine might choose a communications vehicle that I pay attention to most. I listen to musical lyrics with ears like a rabbit. I devour every word, enamored with the puzzle that makes up a song. Ordinary words strung together in extraordinary ways. I am in awe of the writers who start with a blank page and create words that influence and, in this case, change my life.

I know, this may sound like an exaggeration, but it's not. I take my musicals very seriously and this is as serious as a heart attack. I listened and tried to let go of the internal dialogue, instead jumping into the dialogue and lyrics as they played out right before my eyes. As Liz (Elizabeth) walks through her life decisions in scenarios, she can see *if* she does this, *then* she gets that. It's an emotionally charged story that touches on free will, spiritual alignment, friendship, love and, of course, heartbreak. You can't have love without heartbreak.

By the last scene I'm in tears. I can see myself in this story, feel the if/then scenarios playing out in my own life. I look around and I'm sure I'm not alone. There are couples and groups of women of every age. I wonder if any of these people also feel like the stage is coming alive with their fears and indecision.

Every scene feels deeply personal and the finale rings true with every syllable ...

Cause we're always starting over
Every life we're living
Yes, we're always just awake
Every step we take
And my love, I'll make you one last vow

To start over
And over
And over
Somehow
My new life starts right now

My life starts right now. That's how I feel as we drive home. There is no fear, which is a feeling that I don't entirely recognize. I know that big change is on the horizon, I just don't know what is changing. I would prefer to know what I'm going to do, but I know that it's going to be huge, if I can just let myself see it, feel it and make something happen.

I know that my marriage is the first on the list and I don't know when or what I'm going to do. But after being guided by musical wisdom, I have no choice. There is no going back. I decide to try something different.

I notice two things. These strange things happen when I'm either in need of reassurance or to tell me I'm on the right path. So I make a mental note to stay awake and listen.

Chapter 11

Recent Searches:

- Joy from Inside Out image
- Sally from the Grinch image
- Is it bad luck to end a marriage on Halloween?
- How to stop a bloody nose
- Visions of large dogs and wedding rings

The pumpkins are sitting out on the porch, uncarved. The candy bowl was just filled an hour ago and I'm working on hair and makeup, searching for a bobby pin with my left hand while my right hand attempts to wrap a ponytail around a hot bun.

One is dressed as Joy from "Inside Out" and the other is Sally from the "How the Grinch Stole Christmas." Both look adorable and I'm trying hard to fight back the tears. Something's different today. I slept in, which rarely happens, especially on a school day. I felt like I needed the rest and my emotions are heightened. Not because it's Halloween, although to me, this holiday seems busier than Christmas. I have spent all week planning a class party, making the food and organizing the games and music. Since my kids go to a public school, there are no Christmas parties, so all festivities are jammed into Halloween.

Mom and dad are in town from Illinois and are excited to go trick-or-treating with me and the girls. Things are tense in our house.

I go back upstairs to grab my things to go out with the kids and my room looks strange. Empty. There is nothing on his dresser, there are no clothes on the floor. I open his dresser drawer and I feel panic. It's empty. Every last sock gone. I feel panic rising. What does this mean?

I calmly walk down the stairs, "Mom, can you please take the kids out to a few houses and I'll catch up to you?"

She sees that there is something wrong and I see alarm in her eyes, too, but she says nothing and guides the kids out the door. I open the basement door and brace myself for battle.

"Why are all of your things out of the bedroom?" I ask realizing how stupid this question sounds.

"Well, I have moved everything down here," he says as easily as "I took out the trash."

I don't respond, just stand there looking at him with tears streaming down my face. I search for any sign of emotion on his face, but there's nothing so I cry harder, turn around and walk back up the stairs.

The rest of the night goes like all other Halloween nights, but there is something brewing and it's not the apple cider with dry ice that Michaela makes every year for the kids at the end of the night. I'm walking behind a big group of kids with a few other parents. They're talking about soccer and the upcoming school activities. My mom walks with the kids for a bit and then we get to my friend Sydney's house. They're all decked out with a haunted house on their front porch and it looks like they have a full house. Food and drinks flowing. She insists we come in.

The kids run to the basement as fast as they can to be with their friends and my mom and I stand in the kitchen. I introduce her around the room. All couples that we used to hang out with are here. No invites for us over the last year since things have been strained and my health failing. I try to participate in the conversation, but I can't. I ask a question and then it goes flat. I have nothing to say and can't connect, which is rare for me. My mom is talking to someone dressed like a tiger. Normally, I would be lobbying to stay, pouring a glass of wine and settling into the neighborhood gossip. I can't even image that right now. I feel like the room is closing in on me and that I want to run. The music is too loud and the elevated hum of a dozen meaningless conversations is making my head pound. I have to leave. Now.

I walk down the stairs, asking the kids to come up and I pull Sydney aside and whisper,

"Thank you so much for inviting us in, but I have to go. I don't want to go into detail, but things are not good at home and I just can't be here right now."

She hugs me and says over and over how much she supports me and that she's sorry that things aren't going well. She's loving and supportive, telling me to call her if I need anything. Of course, I never have and don't have any intention of doing so.

When I walk in the door, he's sitting on the upholstered chair that my parents bought us last Christmas. It's cream colored with a leafy pattern; the green, blue and brown of the leaves caught my eye when I saw a pair of them at American Furniture Warehouse. Since the room is small, I went with one. It was an attempt to make the place feel like home. Sounds crazy after 10 years in the same house, but I just didn't ever feel settled here.

The kids are in bed and it's nearly midnight. I'm exhausted but I know that this is the time to say what I have to say. I hesitate, consider backing out and sneaking up to bed. But a tingle down the left side of my body and an overwhelming feeling of peace give me the courage I need to stand firm on the maple hardwood floor where I'm standing, facing him. He's not looking at me, instead he's looking over his left shoulder at the TV. I turn my head, too, and I watch for a few minutes as Rachel Maddow gives her debrief of the day's political news.

"Will you please turn the TV off? I want to talk," I say, now looking directly at him. I feel calm and still, my voice is strong and clear and it feels like I'm watching my lips moving, my hands gesturing and listening to my voice about to say words that I know are true, but a truth I have been unwilling to acknowledge. I've thought them, but have never said anything like this out loud.

"It has been a rough year for both of us. I will not live like this anymore," my words are steady, but there is aggression behind them. I can feel warmth moving up from my heart to my chest. The skin burning red there. He says nothing, just looks through me. There is no sign of emotion, but I can feel the rage in him, too.

I continue, "It's time to make a change; we need to separate."

This is not the first time these words have been spoken in some form. Each of us dancing around the "D word" for months. Threatening it, yet both terrified of such a destructive move and how it will affect the kids. But this time is different. There is no going back.

Emotion is now rising up, mixing with the aggression. The heat is rising and I want to scream and cry, but I swallow it down instead when I see his face remaining unchanged.

"I agree," he finally responds after what feels like an eternity.

This is not the reaction I was expecting. I had played out all the scenarios in my head. One was agreement, but it was agreement with a fight or even a plea for another try.

These simple words alone feel like a stab to the heart. But there is also relief. Like I've been waiting for this stab, so that I can pull out the knife and finally begin to heal. I know he's hurting, too; I can feel it. I start to cry, but it's controlled, not my typical hysteria when we have this discussion.

"Ummm," he says, wiping at his nose. Oh my God, is he telling me I have a bat in the cave? Now? What a terrible time for humiliation. I reach my hand to cover my nose and I feel it start to gush. Bright red blood dripping onto my hand.

My cue to walk away I guess. So I run up the stairs holding my nose and my breath. There is sadness, but I feel stronger somehow.

I undress and get into the shower. My therapist always says, "Find water anytime you feel afflicted. Wash the negativity off and let your body, your spirit, flow like the water." I let the hot water wash over me.

Blood is streaming from my nose down my body, pooling at my feet. I hold my nose at the bridge and put my head forward in an effort to slow down the pace, but it seems to be picking up speed. I give up, I let go and let it bleed. I stand there, unmoving, until the water starts to cool. The red water eventually turns pink and then to clear.

I feel cleansed. Free.

I go to bed in a state of shock. Inhale, grace. Exhale, praise. I go through my breathing mantra over and over again. I don't know where it came from, but it has become my ritual as I fight my monkey mind and plead for sleep.

I feel the same peace I felt just weeks before when the weird, slinky light paid me a visit. There is light hovering, but this time just above my bed. Hovering above my feet so I sit up to look closer. The light is dancing, a thick fog morphing into something and I have to blink twice to be sure my eyes aren't playing tricks on me

It's a giant golden dog made of light. Its hair is shaggy. Its sitting, doing that dog smile kind of thing. Tongue flapping, tail wagging and gigantic. But she (I'm assuming it's a she because I prefer female dogs) is friendly, filled with joy. I don't feel intimidated even though she's towering over me, taking up all the space between my bed and the ceiling fan that's whipping around, a draft of air constantly twirling to help me curb the sweating. I feel complete peace and joy and I have no idea why. I'm staring into the dog's eyes; they're familiar, feel like home. Then there's a gentle nudge, not a voice, but a message that I feel rather than hear. Like a sixth sense, it's a knowing deep through my soul whispering, "Look down, to the left." So I do. This is so strange, but my logical brain is nowhere to be found, I just follow the calling.

A twinkling light radiates from my left ring finger. It's been bare for the last six months, but now fractures of light beam up into my eyes, leaving me feeling even more peaceful. I bask in the twinkling light and then lie back down and fall asleep. It's a sweet, deep sleep like I'm being cradled in the arms of angels, rocked to a gentle lullaby.

Chapter 12

Recent Searches:

- Dr. Knight, Colorado
- How to write a book for dummies
- Airfare to Hawaii
- Airfare to Ireland

"If you're here for a diagnosis, then you're in the wrong place," Dr. Knight says as he reviews my file.

He puts it down dismissively and says to me very slowly, "You need to really hear this. You are healthy. Yes, there are some acute symptoms, but you are well and will heal yourself, I'll just give you a little guidance."

I called him a week ago. His name and number scribbled on a yellow Post-It note. It was holding my place on page five of "The Wisdom of the Enneagram," a book recommended by our couples therapist. *This* would be the last doctor I dialed, I promised myself. Just 15 minutes into our meeting and I'm starting to think I may be right.

I'm in his office for more than three hours. We cover it all — diet, nutrition, lifestyle, medications. Standard questions, but he goes deeper, talks about how my emotional and spiritual health are just as important as physical health. He orders blood work and other tests, including genetic testing so that he can, "See what's happening at a cellular level."

He prescribes a medication to take care of the autoimmune reaction in my body, a load of supplements, a reasonable diet adjustment and teaches me how to "breathe correctly and meditate." I'm honest, telling him that I'm too busy to meditate and it's true. I can't commit to it, but I promise, "Yes, I'll keep it in mind and will try to do that once things slow down in my life."

"That's just fine, but it seems to me that you've been pushing yourself too hard for too long. The test results I see in this file," he bangs his hand on it. "They show the signs of a well-meaning mother living in fight or flight."

"Do something for yourself. I know it's hard as a mother, but just like you're instructed in an airplane emergency, you have to put your mask on first so you can help your children." And, with that, he turns and walks away.

As I drive home I'm still reeling about what happened in the night. I have no idea what's going on. Is it happening to me or am I creating it? I feel like I'm being stalked by the friendliest of ghosts. Or there is an invisible director overseeing my life, giving me the cues — gently telling me what to say and where to be.

"Move a little this way and no, don't go too far there or you will fall (and I'm kind of tired of picking you back up all the time)," she might say. The direction is so faint and gentle that it's easy to miss. I even question if it's just my busy mind bullying me around. But there is no doubt that it's there. It's louder today; I'm guessing as a result of my encounter with the cloud of light dancing around my room last night.

I don't tell anyone, well, except for Jamie. The encounter feels too special to share with people who don't share my DNA. I don't want to risk sounding like a lunatic or jinxing whatever is happening, so I hold it close. The only thing I can conclude is that it's a "Casper the Friendly Ghost" kind of thing. This spirit is guiding me and I have a feeling that she has finally had enough of my moping around and indecision, so she's stepping it up and taking matters into her own hands. I start to get curious and notice the things that are happening or the words spoken to me by the people closest, even strangers.

I stop at Starbucks, order a venti iced soy green tea latte, my latest Starbucks obsession. I fire up my laptop and stare at the wireless connection screen as it connects and think about my to-do list that's been piling up over the past several weeks as I've recovered from surgery. I'm aware that this is exactly the opposite of what Dr. Knight has just instructed me to do, but I can start doing things for myself once I get a bit caught up.

No such thing as a break from parenting, even when you're down for the count. I'm still cooking, cleaning, monitoring their screen time, driving them to soccer and piano, and handling the cumbersome bedtime routine. Granted, all of it has been at a slower pace, but with two active kids, life goes on, through sickness and health.

First task: updates to the communications plan for my client. I open my PPT file and the Excel file and I stare at them. My brain rejects them both and the rest of me is in alignment. Just looking at the 50-page PPT and the spreadsheet full of numbers and formulas, I feel bored and desperately want to go home and crawl back into bed. I stare at a slide outlining the five key guiding principles of communications. I read it over and over, but I'm frozen, unable to add to the text box under "Simplicity," where I'm supposed to update the programs in place to simplify the messaging. I just can't do it. So I stare at it harder, willing the words to update themselves.

As I sit still, not speaking or doing, I feel that familiar voice rising up through me. It says, "Write."

"Write," again, the feeling a little bolder. So I open up a Word document and start typing. The words are flying onto the page. I have no objective, no story in mind. I just type and keep typing. There is no effort being put in here, my hands are on autopilot and I feel complete freedom and peace with each word. I would like to say that I created a masterpiece that was later published, but that's not true.

The outcome of the manic typing is a short story about me as a child. It was introspective and a little dark; my earliest memory of a panic attack. This was a memory that vaguely popped into my consciousness on rare occasions, so I was surprised to find out how I really felt about it as the words bled out of me like an open wound. I felt healed and happy when I realized that I had been sitting at Starbucks for two hours.

I'm driving back home and can still feel the leftover buzz of the experience and then the voice rises up again. This time it gives me direction that I had to question and it was loud, very loud. "Write a book," it said, as clear as the blue sky above me, not a cloud to be seen. I laugh at it. It didn't like that. So I heard even louder, deeper, fuller, "Write a book. This is not a joke."

I stop laughing and decide to talk back this time, plead my case. "OK, voice or whatever you call yourself," I say out loud, looking around the car, unsure where to direct my commentary. "Telling me to write a book is ridiculous. Yes, I write a bit for work, but just marketing materials and presentations, things like that. So, no, I'm not writing a book; pretty sure you have the wrong girl."

"Write a book," still gentle, but firm. And then I feel the same peace and joy I felt back at that corner table at Starbucks and during my nighttime wake up calls. "Write a book," washed over me completely, filling the spaces in my body and I felt still, like I was accepting it. So I questioned more.

"OK, voice, what do I know about writing a book? I don't even have a publisher." I say, laughing like I'm talking to an old friend.

The response was quick-witted and clear, "Well, I didn't have a publisher either and my book is the greatest book of all time."

A week later "Amie: Hawaii Writer's Retreat" is written in red dry erase marker on the giant calendar that's taped up on the back of the pantry door with masking tape. My friendly ghost is working overtime. Continuing to point me in the right direction, as long as I'm quiet enough to listen. My first trip on my own, just me. Dr. Knight would be proud, I think.

But I don't stop to think, I just do. Just as I did following my strange and exilirating writing session in Starbucks. Whatever happened in that Starbucks seemed to have stuck to me in the same way the smell of espresso soaked into the fiber of my jeans. There seems to be a threshold for Starbucks sitting, if I'm there for an hour, the smell seems to fade away. If I'm there over two hours something happens to lock that coffee smell in, maybe an intentional move for repeat business? Like if I smell like it, I'll want more. Worst case, I'm guilted into buying more in order to explain the lingering smell of stale coffee beans. Just two days after my Starbucks session, yes the smell hovered, but even more powerful was the chain of events that happened without any effort from me. Two days later I sat on a lounge chair overlooking the neighborhood pool. The girls splashed around in the deep end with their friends while I desperately tried to connect to wifi over and over again, just to be kicked off continuously. An endless cycle of non-working time guilt and exhileration for the ability to be like the other moms, hanging at the pool.

I finally gave up, laying back in the chair and tipping my head back to feel the sun beating down on my cheeks. I hadn't even broken a sweat when suddenly something blocked the rays of light. I slowly open my eyes and I see a bright white smile under a big black sunhat looking down at me instead of the sun.

"Amie!" she sang, reaching down to hug me.

It took my eyes a few minutes to adjust but I looked up to see her tall, lean figure surrounded by rays of light, the sun literally lighting her up.

"Nikki!," I finally said, still mesmerized by the dancing light.

Her daughter the same age as Emma, we became friends over the years when we bumped into each other at school holiday parties and fundraising events. On the rare occasion we got to talk, we didn't skim the surface, we talked about the deep things in life and this day was no exception.

"What's your dream?" she asked, just as easily as someone who asks to please pass the ketchup.

I had never been asked that question or thought about it before. Ever. So I surprised myself by answering quickly, "write a book."

"No way! She exclaimed and sat straight up, swinging her long brown legs over the side toward me. "Well, my best friend just wrote her fourth book and has a new literary agent. I should introduce you two."

And she did. I found myself dialing into Zoom calls every Monday night with her friend who quickly became a friend of my own. We talked about books, story structure and she encouraged me to figure out things like "how Amie writes a book." She introduced me to Angel, her agent and the two took me under their wings. Our calls continued as I stabbed away at a first draft, writing at night when the kids were sleeping. Then one Monday night Angel crooned in her half Australian half Californian accent, "Amie, please join us in Hawaii for the women's writing retreat." To my astonishment I heard my own voice reply without hesitation, "HELL YES!"

I have never done anything like this for myself. Ever. Especially since becoming a mom. All my energy and money going toward my family, which I still believe is the right place for it to be. But as I look at flights from Denver to Kauai, I'm feeling a rush of excitement that I'm not sure I've ever felt. I feel free, exhilarated, yet at the same time, completely terrified. There is a fight between my higher, new-and-improved self and the scared self that cowers within.

"Go, spread your wings. Go after this dream to show your girls how to live, the gentle voice politely suggests. The voice feels like a feather tickling my arm, soothing and calm.

"You have no business spending over $1,000 on airfare; do you know that will cover half of the soccer costs for the year? What kind of mother are you?" the accusing voice booms.

But my higher self puts up a fight that I've never seen before. She picks up speed and takes action ... chooses her seats, paying extra for more leg room and clicks purchase before the scared little girl inside can throw a fit.

I'm shaking as I struggle to remove my strappy sandles in security, the line piling up behind me. A giant man in a Broncos shirt balancing two gray bins breathes down my neck, the lingering smell of tobacco and something alcoholic hits my nose and I nearly lose my balance. Tears are welling up in my eyes and I can feel the anxiety rising.

But once on the island, I'm completely relaxed. Mesmerized by the banyan trees that create a natural path to the beach just beyond my quaint plantation cottage. I walk toward the sea every morning, the gentle Hawaiian breeze blowing my new highlights away from my face. I miss my kids, but I feel free, healthy. I do little to no writing while on this retreat, but I do spend a lot of time thinking about what I might write about in this book that I've been instructed to write. I don't know exactly but I do know that my protagonist will go to Ireland to find her roots and herself.

"Aloha" my shirt reads. I blend with the other mainland tourists walking around the Honolulu airport. I had 12 hours to kill here until my flight departs for Denver. Yes, 12. So I walk, I shop, I take it all in, trying to absorb every last bit of my island experience and avoid the life and circumstances waiting for me at home. My status had officially changed to "separated" and, while we still lived in the same home, our lives were untangling as we walked around the house pretending like nothing had changed. In many ways, it hadn't. I continued to work from my office down the hall from the kitchen. I made dinner and cleaned up, walked the kids to school. Even washed his laundry, neatly folded it and placed in a laundry basket that I would carry down the stairs and place in his makeshift bedroom in the basement guest room.

"Nesting," I had suggested. We rent an apartment and take turns staying in the house with the kids. I was reading two books on divorce. One practical approach to dealing with splitting up a family and one about how to consciously "uncouple" as Gwyneth Paltrow eloquently modeled through her public divorce.

When I finally arrive home the next morning, it's bittersweet. I missed the kids so much but our living situation is getting to me. The girls run out to greet me as I unload my luggage from the back of the Uber, a silver Honda Accord driven by a very sweet Mexican immigrant. Raúl explained to me that he was driving for Uber and

Lyft in order to supplement his income as a manager of a local restaurant. He tells me about his children, one in law school and the other graduated from high school with honors.

"I saved up to send them to University, something I was never able to do," he says proudly. His accent is thick but I can clearly hear the pride and feel the devotion to his family. To me he sounds more American than anyone I've encountered today.

A tingle runs up my left leg. It's now a familiar sensation. I smile and decide to notice it this time, ask it some questions. In my head, of course. I don't want Raúl to think I'm nuts and drop me off at the next exit.

First, I take notice of what's happening in my body. I feel relaxed and I know that I need to stay that way, not tense up. Tensing up is what I do best, especially when there is a weird sensation running up half of my body.

Instead of letting my thoughts free fall into a tornado of alarm, I stop the them in their tracks, take a deep breath and try something new. He's still talking. I think I hear him rattle off how much he has in his 401K and he pauses to think about how much he has in his other savings accounts and I take some deep breaths. In for four, out for four and I close my eyes to tune in, focusing on the sensation in my body.

There is nothing. I no longer hear his voice after he says, "I think I have about $50,000 more in other savings accounts ..." then nothing, not even the noise of the car or the traffic passing by on the highway.

Stillness comes over me, then I hear a whisper. It's faint, even quieter as I strain to hear it better. It's fading and I'm grasping for it. The more I grasp, the further away it floats. Another breath, in for four, out for four, quiet again. This time the whisper is clearer, a bit louder. Like the other times, it's not a sound, but more like a feeling that comes over me as clearly as someone shouting or shoving the information into me. Not just into my brain, but into every cell of my body.

"Tell him that his father must be proud." The voice, or whatever it is, commands.

So without thinking, I blurt out, "Your father must be proud." My voice is loud, it startles me and clearly Raúl, too. He looks back at me even though he's going 75 and should be watching the road. His face is serious, shocked.

"Thank you," he says quietly, turning his head back to the pavement, flashing by in streaks of gray and yellow. I say nothing because I really want to follow the mysterious whatever it is that keeps sending chills up my body and is very clear about what I need to say and do.

"My father died just last week and he never got a chance to tell me he was proud," he says, filling the space with so much love and sorrow that tears sprung instantly to my eyes. Although I couldn't see his eyes, which were steadily watching the road, glancing at the side mirrors as he navigates his way west toward the horizon and my house.

We sit in silence and I check my phone. I smile as I read a new text from my friend, Katherine.

"Amie, I'm going to Ireland this summer. Come with me!"

Chapter 13

Recent Searches

- How to file for divorce
- Jefferson County Courthouse stairwells
- What does seeing 11:11 a lot mean?
- 917 area code

The thud of the metal stamp hitting the divorce decree suddenly brings me out of my all-too-familiar brain fog. I turn to the right and take a look around, doing my best to take it all in. Drink it in like I would any event that is momentous or in this case, life altering. His shoulder is just inches away from mine, a reminder that we're essentially the same height, me a little taller in heels.

It's always a bit of a shock; in my eyes, he towers over me. He's wearing his usual uniform of expensive suit, blue tie and charming smile as he stares at the county worker, willing her silently to move faster. My heart takes a dive again, just as it did at least 10 times on my drive to the Jefferson County Courthouse. I fought back tears and nearly drove home twice as I scoured for parking and then finally ran up the stone steps.

"How did we get here?" I say to myself again and then I realize that this time I actually said it out loud. My voice echoes in the giant, marble-covered room that's surprisingly quiet although it's filled with people. Nothing but an undertone of hushed conversations and sadness hanging in the air. He turns, his eyes bulging, his mouth twitches into something that resembles a frown but nearly a smirk. "We're not going to have this discussion again." Then he turns away from me, a clear sign that I know well. He is done. Checked out.

The clerk is shuffling through the mounds of paperwork, scanning to be sure they were completed. Her eyes buzz up and down and up and down again. I can feel her coldness, her indifference to us and to her thankless job. She goes through the motions without an ounce of emotion, not even a twinge of sadness when she sees that we've been married more than 10 years on page three of the case information sheet. Just another day of work in her eyes. She has likely seen this scenario hundreds of times before. The same sad box checked, "The marriage is irreconcilably broken." Just another day's work, an 8-hour shift closer to the next paycheck.

I can't blame her, she probably has a family to feed and this was likely not her idea of a dream job. I lean forward to take a look around her computer and see a small framed photo of two young boys smiling back.

One is missing his two front teeth, showing off his gums proudly. The other, maybe four years old, is giggling, dimples on both chubby cheeks. They're wearing matching shirts and as I stare at the youngest, fresh tears come springing to my already swollen eyes. Such joy and innocence in his eyes, a stark contrast to the dread that's taken up residence here.

"OK, you'll have to take this slip upstairs to Barb for review. You're missing the petition for dissolution form. Didn't your attorney tell you to fill it out?" just a hint of judgement in her voice.

I feel defensive, finally someone to take my anger out on so I snap back, "Our attorney told us to fill out the 500 forms that are completed, which you have already stamped the life out of and approved. If there is another form, please give it to us and we will fill it out right away."

Now it's her turn, but she decides to play it safe and stay professional. "If I had the form, I would give it to you. You have to go upstairs to the fourth floor and see Barb. Thank you, have a nice day."

I was hoping for a chance to argue that, wanted to say, "no we didn't need to fill out another form thank you very much." I have spent the last two months looking at forms, willing them to complete themselves. And now that I have finally found the strength and courage to take this step, she is now forcing me to take another.

Everyone keeps telling me that I just need to put one foot in front of the other and keep moving on. Well, I'm done taking the steps, I need this part to be complete so I can make my way back to my apartment where I can go back to bed for eternity. We walk together in silence out of the Family Circuit Clerk room and into the hall to find our way to Barb.

I look down the hall and see a bank of elevators but no stairs. Panic starts to ripple through my chest. I close my eyes and take a deep breath.

"Excuse me, can you tell me where the stairs are please?" I ask the police officer standing next to the metal detector at the entrance. He looks confused, like he's never heard this question before. He speaks slowly and I recognize a hint of a Chicago accent, "Ummm, I don't know. I guess there are stairs somewhere but most people just take the elevator; it's right in front of you."

I open my mouth to respond, but nothing comes out. I nod, then walk quickly past the elevators and down the hall, determined to find a stairwell even though I may be the only person who has ever come through the doors of this facility and decided to walk stairs instead of ride a metal box of death.

Who does he think he is, judging me? Maybe I'm a health fanatic and I need the exercise or what if I was an Orthodox Jew and today was the Sabbath, then what? Would he maybe make a gesture to help me find the stairs? Panic has now traveled its way up to my neck; it's burning red and my heart is pounding.

My thoughts swirling and repeating, "I will not get on that elevator." I see a door that looks promising, I pull down on the handle and tug lightly, then again harder. It's locked. Then I try another and another, all with the same outcome.

My breath is shallow and tears are streaming down my face. I'm running down the hall searching for a door that I know doesn't exist.

Maybe this is a sign to not move forward with this; I could walk out the door and not look back.

My heart starts to slow down and I compose myself. As I take a step toward the exit I hear a voice, a whisper that is clear and beautiful, "Get on the elevator, you are going to be OK." I look around, I'm alone in the hallway. The police officer is at least a hundred feet from where I stand. It's just me, surrounded by locked doors and empty courtrooms.

Peace fills my body from head to toe, working its way into every crevasse of my body and deep into my soul. I walk with a mission toward the elevators and push the button to go up.

A ding, the brushed nickel double doors open and I take a brave step inside. Then that same sweet whisper, "Look at your phone." I dig it out of my suede camel bag and look down at the shattered screen. 11:11 it flashes at me and I'm not sure why, but this is soothing and I notice that my breathing is back to normal, in and out, full, deep breaths that I feel completely grateful for.

The doors close and I'm alone in the elevator with wood paneling and mirrors on three sides. I hit the fourth floor button and watch as the building passes by. There is no hint of claustrophobia taking over me. I wait for the walls to start closing in on me and my breath to stall, but nothing. I'm OK. There is a knowing that comes over me that I can't put my finger on. I'm not afraid of the bottom falling out and plummeting to my death or being trapped in this very small space forever. Four lights up and I come to a stop, the doors open and I know that I have to take this last step over the small crack in the floor that separates me from this confined area of stale air and solid ground. I take the step and don't look back.

He's waiting for me just outside the elevator. He looks up for a second as I walk off the elevator, then back to his phone, typing ferociously. I can tell that it's important and his eyebrows are crinkled in the way they always are when he's frustrated. Without looking up, he starts walking toward the office of Barb Kippinger, her name to the right of the glass door on a gold plaque. I notice that my shoulders have dropped, my stride is longer, more confident than it has been in weeks, maybe months. Somehow, I feel lighter than I have in longer than I'm willing to admit.

A receptionist takes our case number and the slip of paper and we wait in silence in the flowery arm chairs that look like they belong in my grandma's house, which hasn't been updated in a century.

The chair is surprisingly comfortable and while I expect it to smell musty, instead I'm overcome with the strong smell of lavender. It's a gorgeous smell, soothing and pleasant, but so strong that it's nearly burning my nose. Does he smell it, too? I wonder. If he does, I would never know because he's still entranced by his mobile device, the typing and brow furrowing now at a much higher level of intensity.

I start to ask him, but decide to say nothing as the receptionist calls our names, "Case Number 234, Barb will see you now."

We walk into Barb's office, him 10 steps ahead of me. Strangely, I notice that her office also smells of a very large lavender field and that the calmness that poured over me on that elevator was still lingering all around me like a force field, a bubble of contentment that not even my soon-to-be-ex-husband could break. I mouth a "thank you" to the sky and hold my breath a little as I settle in for round two of paperwork roulette.

When I come out of Barb's office there's a missed call. I don't recognize the number and there's no voicemail. I sit down on a bench near the elevators and google the area code. My stomach turns, it couldn't be. After all this time? I tap the number in my phone to call back.

His voice is booming and memories flood back as he says, "Amie, I'm so happy to hear your voice, I have been waiting four years for this call. Thank you for returning my call."

"Jonathan, why are you calling me?" I ask.

"Darling, you know why I'm calling. My feelings haven't changed. When you meet your soulmate, those feelings don't just go away. Even after all this time," his words so intimate that I feel tears rising.

"I don't know what to say, but I do want you to know that I'm in the process of a divorce," I say abruptly. Not really an appropriate response to what he has just shared, but I'm angry that he can still be playing this game.

"Oh, I'm so sorry, are you OK?" he asks, I can hear sincerity in his voice and I soften my stance.

"I'm sorry, this is really hard for me, I was naïve and really felt like we had a strong connection and I'm embarrassed that I fell for that," I surprised myself with the directness of my statement.

"Embarrassed? I'm the one who's embarrassed. I fell hard for you, Amie, and I'm sorry that I caused such heartache for you, I only want what's best for you. What I said to you, the way I feel for you is real and I don't understand why you don't believe it. It's the truth," his voice is quiet.

I say nothing because I'm crying, fighting hard to hide it.

He continues, "Please don't cry. I love you and that has not and will not change. Did you get the book I sent?"

Chapter 14

Recent Searches

-   What time is it in Dublin?
-   Is it rude to order English breakfast tea in Ireland?
-   Cal, Irish actor

I should be jet-lagged, but instead I only feel energized when I open my eyes. My cell phone is on the fluffy white pillow to my left. It's 10am Dublin time. I jump up, ready to take in our first day. The room is still dark, blinds drawn and Katherine isn't moving yet. She pulls the covers higher over her and rolls toward the wall and I head to the bathroom to shower, tiptoeing so I don't wake her up.

We made a pact that we would let each other sleep. Our number one mission of this trip is to rest and relax. Number two mission is to have an Irish experience full of sights, pints and, God willing, a few men to kiss and flirt with along the way.

We landed in Dublin at 5am today, survived the drive from the airport to the hotel, my first time driving on the wrong side of the road. I white-knuckled it as Katherine acted as my personal navigation system, reminding me on every turn to stay to the left as she saw the front of our tiny red car veer right. She saved our lives and I said prayers that we would arrive at our first of many boutique hotels alive.

This trip couldn't have come at a better time. The divorce hearing was held one month ago and I received the legal documents in the mail just a week before I flew out. I expected it to feel more ceremonious, but it didn't. It felt sad and like nothing.

So here we are and I am excited to get started on my writing and have my first cup of Irish tea. I walk down the rose velvet lined hallway, decorated with modern art and funky mirrors and down the stairs to the hotel restaurant.

There is a sign, "Seat Yourself Please" so I choose a table set for two by the window. My back to the rest of the restaurant, nestled by the corner of the bar.

The Morrison Hotel seems to be the hot spot for Sunday morning brunch. It's contemporary and cool. I thought this would be the case by looking at the room rate and photos online, but I couldn't be sure. With its close proximity to Temple Bar and Grafton Street, it was the obvious choice as I tried to find just the right spot in Dublin to kick off our trip. Since this was the first vacation I had ever planned, I wanted to go all out, spare no expense. There would be no two-star hotels for this adventure — top notch all the way.

I order the Irish farm breakfast: two eggs any style, ham and toast. "Coffee or tea?" the waiter asked but not in an Irish accent like I expected. He sounded and looked Mediterranean. Italian maybe?

I open up my laptop and start typing randomly in chapter two of my manuscript.

I'm distracted by the pure magic of being here, so I stop typing and I stare out the window instead. The minute I'm on Irish soil, I feel grounded and steady. It feels like coming home. Yes, my ancestors on my mother's side came to the US from Ireland, but that was generations ago. I don't know if it's a genetic pull or the pull of the Irish spirit. We're all attracted to it. The friendly banter, the happy-go-lucky way of life, or the personalities of the people and their greatest pastimes of drinking, telling stories and music.

When you're there, you want to be a part of it. It feels welcoming, like family. And when you're not there, you feel left out, like you're missing a party.

Here I am, in the middle of the party. Dead center in Dublin and, even though I haven't even been here 24 hours, I'm sure that I will never want to leave.

I fill my dainty china tea cup with more hot water and then look over my shoulder as I see that two men, one of them very cute, are being seated right behind me. I don't understand this since the part of the restaurant I'm sitting in is nearly empty. There are at least 10 other tables at which they can be seated.

Maybe the waiter is lazy and doesn't want to have to walk the extra steps to take their order while continuing to bring me more hot water. I'm sure he can tell that I'll be here awhile. I'm certainly not going to complain. That's not how I roll, especially in a foreign country filled with people pleasers just like me. I will just happily listen to their conversation, maybe they'll give me some good material to write into my manuscript.

The conversation is fast and, with two male Irish accents, it's hard for my American ears to keep up and make out all the words being thrown around. There is a very long series of pleasantries. "How are you, mate, it's great to see you" "Did you find the place OK?" "Oh you did, that's lovely." "Sure is a lovely day today, no rain I see and really glad that this time worked for you" "Ah yes, this time is very good for me as it's a Sunday and my wife goes to her weekend walk and tea with her friends." I noticed that the cuter one didn't talk about having a wife; that piqued my interest.

Then they were off to the objective of this meeting. "So, tell me more about this idea of the documentary, I would be very interested indeed," said the cute one whose back is to mine, our chairs almost touching. His chair so close that I thought he was going to sit with me.

"Ah, yes, well, I have contacted a few of the authors I know here in Dublin and I have some interest," says the one who is married, he has dark hair and is much shorter than the other one from my 10 second appraisal of the two. I sneak a peek behind me to see that the single one has blondish curly hair, his head resting on the back of the ivory upholstered chair and his legs stretched out in front of him, a low black lacquer table between them.

He speaks and I quickly turn my head back to my laptop, "Well done, well done. Yes, that sounds grand. The idea is that I would interview them, is it?"

I notice that at the end of every sentence their voices rise up into a question. I wonder if this is an Irish thing, this asking questions that they already know the answers to. So I keep listening to hear if I can prove my theory.

"That's right. Yeah, yeah, you've got it right, lad. I'll handle locking in the writers and doing up the script and you do the front of the camera thing, like you do," says dark haired, married guy.

There is a bit more back and forth on who will do what and some brainstorming, so I go back to my tea drinking and random typing of nothingness. Then I hear some words that catch my attention.

Cute, curly haired blond guy says, louder than his previous conversations, "Now, what if we could find some American writers, maybe a few have written about people or places in Dublin?"

Are they spying on me? Can they see my screen? I guess I have nothing but some random words about my character Leah and some useless dialogue between her and her sister, none of which mentions Dublin or anything Irish.

Is this for real? Maybe I'm being "Punk'd" or the Irish version of the Ashton Kutcher reality show.

"Say something, say something, say something …" the voice inside of me is growing louder and sounds on the verge of hysteria. Is the small, still voice inside of us supposed to lose its patience? I don't think so. But leave it to mine to have no patience and be overly dramatic.

"Excuse me … I'm here from America, just arrived today, and I'm writing a book," I hear myself saying and they both turn to look at me. Friendly smiling faces, nodding and listening.

So I go on, "And I couldn't help but overhear, since they seated you pretty much on top of my table, that you're working on a documentary about writers?"

But, before either of them can answer, I keep talking fast, "and, I just had to speak up because I'm here to write because part of my book will be set in Ireland."

Cute curly blond turns around and oh yes, he is cute! He's wearing glasses, but behind them are bright blue eyes and his jaw is square, distinguished, his smile is sweet and boyish. He's the first to speak up, "No way, that has to be the Universe telling you that you need to talk to us. What is your book about? Is it fiction?"

Was I writing fiction? I have no idea. No clue what this so-called book is about. But that voice, which I now lovingly call God … ever since he put the publisher/Bible card on me, asked me to write it and sent me on a journey to figure it out.

I don't want you to get hung up here. I say God, but you may be comfortable with something else. Call the voice your intuition, or the Universe like cute Irish guy just did. Call it Gus, for all I care. Just be sure to listen to it and be still enough to let it come through because we all have a magical gift inside that conspires for our full happiness.

But I don't say any of that. Instead, I answer, "It's about a woman who goes to Ireland to trace her roots and she finds out some dramatic family secrets and has some adventures along the way," I summarize, leaving out the romantic comedy spin that I include when talking to women.

"Grand, grand, that sounds lovely then," he says smiling, looking at his dark haired married friend who introduces himself as Gerry.

"Oh, where are my manners, my name is Callum, you can call me Cal" he stands up and reaches for my hand.

They both take turns talking to me about the documentary, which is still in concept stage and then Gerry asks for my email address, says he will send me an email so that we can be in touch to interview me when my book is launched. They are "interested indeed" as Cal puts it when we discuss the possibility of an interview.

"I'm the in-front of the camera guy. I'm an actor, so you would get to be on camera with me," he winks at me and my stomach flutters a little. "Ger is the writer and producer," he adds, taking a sip of his tea.

We chat for a bit. They want to know all about my trip and what I plan to do while I'm here. Friendly is an understatement for these two and I'm smiling ear to ear, proud that I was able to speak up. I politely leave them to their business and go back to my laptop, although I feel like we could have kept talking and they wouldn't have minded at all.

Katherine slips into the chair across from me as I start to type. Saved again, I think. So I shut down the laptop and fill her in on the new friends within ear shot. She orders a coffee and we look at our map of Dublin, planning out our day.

I look at my phone and there's already an email there from Gerry with he and Cal's contact information and a sweet note. "What a pleasure meeting you, Amie. Let's make a documentary soon. Cheers!"

The Irish boys are standing, saying their very long, Irish goodbyes. I try to look busy like I'm not listening in. "Don't go, don't go," I'm thinking, willing Cal to stay.

"So nice to meet you, Amie. Enjoy your time in Ireland," Gerry yells, waving and then turns toward a woman standing near the door.

"Oh, goodbye, so nice to meet you," I yell across the room toward his back.

Cal is sitting back down in his chair and I feel relief. "Gerry had to leave to meet his wife, but I'm planning to stay, may I join you?" he asks

I'm smiling and staring at him and it takes me a few seconds to realize that he has asked me a question.

"he, he, he," he laughs. I'm busted.

Chapter 15

Recent Searches

- Killarney car repair
- Is there really only ONE dolphin in Dingle Bay?
- How to pet a sheep
- Urban dictionary – feck
- How to wear a Claddagh ring

I drive the Irish countryside on the wrong side of the road from the wrong side of the car, way too close to the stone walls that line the windy, narrow roads. My hub caps are banged up pretty badly. Katherine navigates from the backseat and she's now on stone wall watch, yelling "stay right" when I get too close.

We have a system as we plug along our route from Dublin to Killarney through Dingle and then up to Galway and back to Dublin again, hitting the sights along the way. The Ring of Kerry, The Cliffs of Moher. We even see Fungi the dolphin in Dingle Bay (look it up, it's for real say the Irish).

"You want to know how the long the Dingle Ring is, do you?" an Irish guy smoking in front of a pub in Killarney answered Katherine when she asked for directions to the Ring of Kerry at 10am on a Tuesday.

His friend joined him on the sidewalk with a pint. "Let me tell you the best route. It's through this door, your best Irish experience is in a pub ladies," he said as his friend lit his cigarette for him.

I take that as an invitation and look at Katherine nodding. No go, she wants to see the Ring and I don't blame her, this is her first time in Ireland. So off we go to scrape up the hub caps and continue our quest to pet a sheep. This trip is my second time in Ireland. The first with the now ex-husband 10 years ago. I have re-created the same trip that we took but with a twist. No tight timelines and we leave time to relax and do what we feel.

"Now, if Katherine wants to pet a sheep she needs to sneak up on him. Tip toe, they're very skittish. You can call me when you're able to stalk one and I'll walk you through it," Cal instructed us over a WhatsApp voice message.

He kept us entertained along the way with his hilarious and really quite useful advice. Our own personal tour guide, even speaking Irish in some of the messages.

"This is an important lesson ladies, so pay attention now. Maybe you should pull over so Amie doesn't further damage the rental car," he said in one particularly long recording.

We exchanged WhatsApp texts and voice message for the next five days as we traveled. No discussion of if or when we would see each other. It didn't matter, we were having fun and we both knew that our paths would cross again. His words are beautiful. Spoken or written, it all sounds like poetry to me. He is sweet, genuine and funny.

Like me, he's on a journey of healing. There is depth to our exchanges and it feels easy, joyful. I'm sitting in front of the fireplace at our sweet Dingle hotel with my laptop open to chapter three of my manuscript. No, I haven't made much progress with all the sightseeing and sheep stalking.

"Hi. How's Dingle?" a message from Cal pops up.

I snap of picture of the fireplace, my feet crossed on the thick pine coffee table.

"That's a five-star fireplace. Desperately looking for the transport button on this phone," he replies right away. Then another. "I'm calling Vodafone, the button is missing, demanding my money back," he replies right away.

"Meet me in Galway on Wednesday," I reply, but I want to take it back. I don't want to sound desperate.

A voice message pops up a few minutes later. I hear his Irish accent, sexier than ever say, "Now if this isn't the Universe conspiring for us, I don't know what is … just today I received a text from my friend asking if I would like to join her in Galway. You won't believe it … on Wednesday. It is meant to be … so it seems."

Us? Did he say us? I'm warm all over and it's not just the flames that are burning a few inches from my toes.

We arrive in Galway on Wednesday morning, walk around Eyre Square towards the Corrib, taking in all the shopping. There are musicians on nearly every corner.

This place is alive, I feel alive. It feels like retracing my steps looking for something I've lost. I walked Quay Street 10 years ago. I don't remember the brightly colored doors lining the street or the sound of music and laughter filling the air. This was before my body imploded on me, so I considered myself relatively healthy at that point. Yet, I do remember walking the streets of Galway with a head that felt fuzzy from antihistamines. "I am allergic to Ireland," I had jokingly said but then promptly sneezed and then itched my swollen eyes.

This time is different. I feel healthy, like my body is working with me rather than against me. There isn't a hint of histamine intruding on me right now. I feel weightless as I walk into Thomas Dillon's Claddagh Gold. "The Original Claddagh" it says above the royal blue door.

They have a huge selection and I've been waiting to get here so I could buy rings as gifts. I buy three: one for Jamie, one for mom and one for me. All sliver, but each a little different style so we could be distinct.

I couldn't wait to put mine on so I stopped right in the middle of the heavy shopping traffic. People bumping into me from every direction as I balanced my shopping bags and put it on my right finger without regard to where the heart of crown was pointing.

I know there is some kind of rule about how to wear a Claddagh, so I google it while we have lunch at Taafe's Bar. According to Irish author Colin Murphy, a Claddagh ring is worn with the intention of conveying the wearer's relationship status. If worn on the right hand with the point of the heart toward the wrist, the wearer is in a relationship. But I decided not to flip it, which would show my newly single status. It just felt right, so it stayed. I look down at the silver heart and crown and I hear that small voice say, "You are in a relationship with you."

The g Hotel and Spa is fabulous. I feel like a celebrity here. The lobby looks like an art museum and our stylish room has a purple couch in front of the window and two cupcakes sitting on an oversized white plate in the middle of a stainless steel coffee table. They're frosted meticulously with chocolate and a white "g" resting on top. Katherine and I are both strictly gluten-free so we can't eat them, but they are beautiful.

I'm stressing over getting ready. It feels like a date. "Is it a date?" I ask Katherine. "No, it's not a date because I'm going with you and so is his friend. You look great, let's go!" she says, holding the door for me and double checking her pocket that she has a key.

I see him standing at the bar looking stylish in khakis, white shirt and a navy blazer. His smile widens when he sees me and I feel immediately relaxed, eager to get closer for a hug.

Introductions are made and the four of us walk out into the Galway night toward the action. His arm brushes up against mine every few minutes; I can feel the electricity.

"I'm here for a medical convention. I'm a heart surgeon and so are all of these drunk people dancing here. But don't worry, they're highly competent when not intoxicated," The Indian American guy points to a group to his right.

He came up to me and Cal as we were dancing, asks if he can take a photo of us. Now that I think about it, that's kind of weird. We find out that he's also from Colorado, the suburb next to mine. So we meet his wife and a few of his colleagues.

We're standing on the smallest dance floor I have ever seen at the Quay Street Pub. A two man band is playing on an elevated stage in front of us. The "dance floor" is about the size of the coffee table in our hotel room. It's a rectangle cut out of the old wood floors and covered in multi-colored glass tiles. A light shines through it from the floor and everyone here is fighting their way to get a turn to show off their dance moves on the small piece of real estate.

Cal and I get the most stage time. We offer others a turn, but the heart surgeons have taken a liking to us and encourage us to take the spotlight. Neither of us can argue with that. We spend the night hand in hand socializing, floating around the pub and then the Galway night, like butterflies. It's just the two of us as we flutter back to the g Hotel.

In the candlelight of the lobby we're face to face, our connection stronger than any I've ever experienced. I have only known him for such a short time, but I've never let anyone get this close.

My heart is in sync with his, beating at the exact same rhythm. So close that I can't tell where he ends and I begin. He's looking into my eyes, but I can tell that he sees more than the face in front of him, swollen lips from a night of kissing, flushed cheeks from dancing. He sees my soul and I see his.

He whispers, "Amie, do you want to make love?"

Chapter 16

Recent Searches

- The Interior Castle, Amazon
- Killiney Hill history
- How do you say love in Irish?
- Love Story Lyrics, Taylor Swift

"It's a love story, baby just say yes," Taylor Swift wails. The speakers are right above our café table at Dublin International Airport.

Our words are unspoken, but lingering above us as we silently sip our tea.

I flew back to Dublin just four weeks after I returned from the first trip. Our connection grew over Zoom calls and WhatsApp messages heated up. The words "I love you" exchanged through recorded voice messages, but more tangible than any other time those words have been spoken face to face.

"Cal, thank you for such an amazing time. I loved being with you and getting a glimpse into your life here. And I also think it's very cool that I got to see Bono's wife pulling into her driveway," I say laughing because he was mortified when I took a picture.

He lives in the same town as Bono. *The* Bono. He grew up here in this beautiful coastal village just outside of Dublin. It's picturesque and sweet, like looking at a postcard, you just want to be there.

We spent hours walking at Killiney Hill Park, hiking to the top, which is crowned by an obelisk. We each made a wish and walked around its ledges, an old Irish tradition.

I sat in the Druid's chair — a chair made of stone where the ancient Celtic priests would sit and train their apprentices. He showed me the ruins sprinkled across the hill that were used for ancient wedding ceremonies. "I want to show you a special place," he said, taking my hand and walking up a narrow trail near the top of the hill. We climbed higher through a patch of gravel and thorny shrubs to a small spot at the very top. Two big rocks rested there and the space directly beneath them made a perfect seat.

From here we had a bird's eye view of the sea and it was breathtaking. Blue as far as the eye could see. "Dublin is there to the South," he points. "This was always my special place when I was growing up. I would climb up here to think, clear my head."

We held hands and stared out into the sea in silence. It was all very romantic. A five day trip that flew by, just as fast and furious as our relationship. The connection was deep and real, both of us commenting things like, "I feel like I've known you forever," the other nodding in astounded agreement. Each day, we slept in late and drank tea in the garden. "Can I put the kettle on for you, darling?" he would ask in an Irish accent thicker than it really was for my American amusement. He taught me how to relax and he was the master of relaxation. There was no washing up after breakfast, the dishes piling up in the tiny white basin sink. Even the trip to the airport was a leisurely one, both of us dragging our feet, wanting to extend the togetherness as long as possible.

"It's strong and it's sudden and it's cruel sometimes, but it might just save your life. That's the power of love. That's the power of love," Huey Lewis sings, the volume seems louder than the boarding announcements that are competiting

"Sorry, I just have to say ... I can't help, but notice the music blaring above us. What the feck is that? It sounds like closing credits to a romantic film and it's corresponding to our conversation," he says through little fits of laughter.

His laugh is contagious. I'm laughing, too. "I was …," I snort. "thinking the same thing and thought maybe it was my imagination," I finally get out in between giggles.

"Since it seems that whomever is orchestrating the music has done a fine job of saying what we wanted to say, I'll just say this, I love you," I say, tears welling up in my eyes.

"Oh baby. Let's stay together (gether), lovin' you whether, whether … times are good or bad, happy or sad …" Al Green is now serenading us.

And with that we just smile at each other. He grabs my hands and kisses them, our eyes locked and asking a million silent questions. This feels like a significant goodbye, almost embarrassing, the drama of it all. The line for security is just 100 feet away from the café, so we walk the short distance hand in hand, slowly putting one foot in front of the other, strides in sync, sneaking glances at eachother. I feel an ugly cry welling up in my throat but I swallow it down, turn toward him and wrap my arms around his neck and bury my face into the blond curls that graze his smooth, tan skin. I'm afraid to let go, to walk away. If I didn't have a hard deadline I could have stood there in his arms forever. But I knew I had to walk away, so I did.

"While I was beseeching Our Lord today … I began to think of the soul as if it were a castle made of a single diamond or of very clear crystal, in which there are many rooms, just as in Heaven there are many mansions. — St. Teresa of Avila"

This quote is highlighted on the back of my book. I pull it out of my laptop bag while I wait to board my flight.

"The Interior Castle by St. Teresa of Avilla is a must read," Mirielle said as she hugged me and slipped the book in my purse at the same time at the end of our first session last week. Mirelle is my new therapist. Yes, I have two. I am not ashamed, in fact I think it's a good thing, I'll take all the good advice and psychoanalyzing I can get. Mirelle was referred to me by a friend of Jamie's who was also going through a divorce. "She is meditative based and helped her through trauma," Jamie told me and then promptly texted me her phone number with clear directions, "Call her. Now." So I did and drove an hour to meet her the next day.

She wore a long white rope with a violet scarf wrapped around her neck, a silver cross shining just beneath it. Her eyes, covered by small circle lensed glasses did more than look at me, she saw through me, right to the core of me and I could feel it immediately. There was no hiding out in the presence of this woman.

She was loving but direct. There was no recapping my childhood, somehow she already knew. In just two hours she guided me through the darkness that plagued me and then up into the light. I don't know how and I don't care. All I know is that I walked out the door of the sanctuary that she called the retreat house feeling 10 pounds lighter.

I turned my head to look at her, "St. Teresa of Avilla wrote a book?"

"Oh honey, yes, St. Teresa wrote many books. She is one of the great mystics," she replied.

"I began to think of the soul as if it were a castle made of a single diamond of very clear crystal, in which there are many rooms, just as in Heaven there are many mansions," St. Teresa of Avila wrote in the first chapter. I'm mesmerized that this is the same woman whose name I wrote down on a piece of paper many years ago. Her words are humble and honest. I like her. I now consider her as my third therapist.

Chapter 17

Recent Searches

- Do pumpkin carving services exist?
- Is buying a house on Halloween bad luck?
- How to take stains out of white quartz countertops
- Handyman nearby

There are pumpkins on the porch. Just like last year, all four are uncarved with no plans to cut into them and pull out the seeds. A tradition we look forward to as a family of four every year, with the exception of the last two. Life has been too busy and emotions too high as we cut our family in two.

I've been thinking about all the good times and traditions we've built in the house we bought together 10 years ago. The girls were just babies and I was walking around in a sleep deprived state going through the stages of newborn to toddler. And then, just as sleep deprived through their first days of kindergarten and the early elementary school years. I'm not tired in that "new mom" kind of way. This kind of tired is stress-induced from working early mornings and late nights so that all the rest of my time revolved around the kids and their activities. Now they are categorized as "tweens" and they surprise me every day. I can see the amazing women they will soon be.

It's all gone by way too quickly. Every parent in a more advanced stage than me always warned, "Enjoy it, it goes by fast." I ignored their well-intended advice, mostly because I didn't believe them because some days, especially during the younger years, felt like an eternity. But now that I'm here, 10 years into parenthood, I understand the wisdom that was being shared with me. It does go fast but I have no regrets and I now understand more than ever the importance of living in the moment. There is an archive of memories. They are sweet and I can feel the essence of each one drift over me as I pack up the last few things I'm taking with me when I move just a mile up the road.

Today is the day. I drive across town to close on my home. The closing officer greets me in the lobby. She's dressed like a black cat, whiskers and all. Since she crossed my path does that mean bad luck, I wonder.

"Happy Halloween," she says as I try to not walk in her path just in case as she leads me to the conference room where my mortgage broker/friend is waiting for me.

There's just one line to sign on each page, no spouse to share the responsibility. She explains as I sign, my friend translating when he can tell that I don't understand. It's a quick process and my stomach twirls with excitement that I will be sleeping in my own room tonight. There will be no furniture for a few days, most being delivered over the weekend. But my own space sounds like heaven. I have been dreaming of this day for a long time. It's hard to believe it's finally here.

She hands me the key. Her black nose crinkles and her whiskers jiggle as she smiles at me and say, "congratulations."

The key chain is ready, has been sitting on my nightstand for close to a year. A thick gold ring with a bright yellow heart dangling from it. "You are a sparkle of light in this world," it says across the front in a flowy font. A gift from a dear friend, this token has been a daily reminder that I will soon have a key to my new life. A chance to build a new home and foundation for me and my girls.

The thick planks of the light wood floors are glowing, the white quartz countertops lined with glass subway tile are glistening and the blingy chandeliers I chose are very "old Hollywood meets shabby chic."

"*This* is where I belong," I say out loud to no one. Although I do hope that my angels know that I am moving. I'm sure that they do, but I call them in just in case.

"Hi. It's me, Amie. Well, you know ..."

"Anyway, I just wanted to let you know that I've moved," I say, jiggling my keys.

"I also want to say thank you for all of your support, it feels like you have been guiding me through this journey and well ... thank you."

I sit down in the middle of the empty room where I envision my white shag rug and glass coffee table will go. I didn't expect divorce. I'm sad that I will never again sleep in the place where I brought my kids home from the hospital. Just the thought of spending the night, let alone half of the time, away from my kids makes me feel like I'm going to hyperventilate.

After trick or treating with the kids that night I go back to the house. It's bare but beautiful. I wash my face in my hotel-inspired bathroom, all white with shiny silver finishes and then into my vaulted-ceiling master bedroom. A twin-sized air mattress is in the corner. I borrowed it from a friend as I prepared for this night.

"This will be fun, like camping out and bonding with my new place," I thought. Tomorrow morning the movers pick up the boxes and the few pieces of furniture I stacked on one side of the garage. Although the divorce decree states, "all household belongings will be split 50/50," I only took the necessities and a handful of furniture. I decided to start over, a new opportunity for a fresh start. Fresh start meant all new towels, sheets, mattresses, even forks. If I had to start over again I wanted to do it on my own terms. This also meant racking up some credit card bills, but it's worth it.

I settle onto the tiny blow up bed. It squeaks as I toss and turn trying to find an air pocket that might help my body relax.

"If this is what divorce looks like, then sign me up," my friend Caitlyn says when she walks in the next morning. She's carrying a vase of bright yellow roses and a venti iced green tea latte. She knows me well, I think, as I laugh and give her a hug. She's joking of course, but she's got a point. The furniture slowly arrives throughout the day and my space is starting to resemble a home.

Is this what divorce looks like for me? All white Ikea dishes and new furniture that's out of my price range?

I guess that's how I "do" divorce. Could be worse, I suppose. Hope I don't have to challenge my theory again. Ever. But, all in all, I think I can take a little credit for carrying it out in style and with very little collateral damage.

I'm trying to enjoy this move but I'm stressed. It feels too monumental, too bittersweet, so I go for a freaked out attitude as I carry in boxes and unpack my kitchen. I'm supposed to be carrying out these tasks mindfully, living in the moment, etc. etc. But I don't feel like it today so I drink loads of caffeine and painstakingly put my stuff away. Jamie, Mary and Constance have all cleared their calendars from sun up to sun down at my beck and call. They are amazing. Not only are they taking charge of whipping the place into shape, they are taking turns counseling me to get through this without a breakdown of some sort. I'm obsessed with getting the girls' rooms set up and making sure that everything looks perfect so they will accept this as their new home. I'm terrified that they won't.

"You're here, that's all they want. That makes it home for them," Constance keeps telling me over and over again. She's right, of course. She's always right when it comes to this kind of stuff, but I just can't hear it, embody it today. I'm scared, so I go back to obsessing over the placement of bed frames and matching clothes hangers.

Scared that I've made all of these decisions by myself and every decision from now on is in my hands alone. I'm not used to making decisions on my own. I wasn't even born on my own, even had a partner for that. So "going solo" just doesn't come naturally to me. In my marriage, he was the decision maker on everything from the finances to the color of the walls, even the number of pillows on the bed. You name it, he picked it. I was happy to oblige for a few years but then the resentment built and I found myself screaming to be heard and then second guessing the voice that croaked out.

I noticed it right before I turned 30. It seems that I have epiphanies approximately once per decade. (Noted for my 50th.) I will be smarter in 10 years' time I hope, and will listen intently *before* it all falls apart. I wish I could have just 15 minutes with the younger me. The me that was working hard to prove her worth to everyone around her, especially herself. The people-pleasing mission in life would be my first topic on the agenda.

"Hey you ... yeah you, the one without a stitch of makeup and the scraggly hair."

When I was newly married, I stopped wearing makeup and didn't get my hair cut or colored for over a year. I'm not a high-maintenance kind of girl, but I always made these things a priority in my life. Until I walked into a quick marriage in a new city with a low paying job and credit card debt. The self-care expenses went out the window and were not even considered for the budget. Slowly, all the things that I liked to do for myself went away, replaced with a new focus on the priorities of my other half. I took self-sacrifice to great lengths. So much so that I didn't even recognize the self in me at all.

It happened gradually, yet all at once. I'm definitely an "all in" kind of girl. So I jumped in head first and didn't even consider speaking up or shifting gears. I've forgiven him and myself for the spiral of self-destruction. Forgiving myself is the hardest part. I still grieve for that time but I know that it was a fall that I needed in order to find my footing once again.

Chapter 18

Recent Searches

- Emergency stress relief meditation
- Symptoms of a heart attack
- Urgent Care near me
- Photo of Jim Gaffigan
- What to do with a dead hedgehog

"... you are safe, your feet are resting on solid ground. Take a deep breath and know that this will pass." My Chromebook is playing the "Emergency Stress Relief" guided meditation for the fifth time since midnight. It's 2am and I don't think I've ever seen the sky so dark. Darkness surrounds me and the only thing I know to be true is that it's going to swallow me up and I'll never see light again

I need out. Out of this bedroom, out of this house. It doesn't even feel like it belongs to me. Not even the blingy chandelier that hangs above my bed. I've been settled in here for more than six months and somehow it has suddenly dawned on me that I'm here alone. ALONE.

My heart hammers in my chest, pounding harder and harder like it's ready for takeoff. It has taxied down the runway and is reaching maximum acceleration. Full throttle. My eyes flutter open and I'm not sure if I've managed to open them because I see nothing but black. Something has happened and I don't know what it is. No memory of a terrible phone call and there are no alarms blaring. Everything is quiet, empty. I'm the only one in the house and then I'm clearly aware that this may be the alarming event.

"I miss the kids," a tiny whisper from deep within rises up and I start to cry.

"How could you have split your family in two?" My brain asks shrilly.

I get quiet, straining to hear my gut, listen for a clue from God, but there is nothing. Just more of the darkness and the rapid "ba-bum, ba-bum, ba-bum" of my heart.

A sharp stab in my chest sends panic through me. My neck feels paralyzed and my throat constricted.

I sit with my legs folded up on my floor and I try to meditate. My brain is having none of this. It's throwing a fit like a two year old so I jump up and grab my phone and dial the last number on my phone.

"Jamie ..." I can barely get her name out in between cries that are shaking my whole body.

"Amie, what's wrong?" she asks in a panic. I can tell that she has jumped out of bed, maybe she fell, I hear a thud.

"I'm ... ok ... no, I'm not really. I think I might be having a heart attack," I trail off, with no idea what I'm going to say, my brain swirling, searching for the options.

"Amie, Amie, are you there?" Jamie screams.

"Yes, I'm here," I notice that my voice is quiet and weak.

She goes on, "OK, I'll be right over?" but she doesn't wait for me to answer and goes on, "You are OK, just take deep breaths. You are OK."

I hang up the phone and lie back down on my bed. It's still dark

I get up and walk around the room, surprised that I'm able to stand on my own two feet without falling down.

"Ahhhhhhhhhhhhh" I wail to no one. Then I cry a cry that I've never know. A cry that comes from the core of my being. It's raw, primal, a voice I've never heard before. It's deep and as it pours out of my mouth, my throat burns. A toxic scream, shooting all the negativity out into my dark and empty room.

"Heart," I hear, the tiny whisper is back but it's faint. I put my hand over my heart and pick up a sweater from the floor with the other, then slip on my fuzzy gray slippers and walk down the stairs.

I walk slowly and with purpose. But I know there is no real purpose. I have no idea what I'm doing or where I'm going. I grab my keys, hanging neatly on the hook by the door, the first thing I hung on my wall when I moved in. I'm holding the yellow heart keychain that hangs from my car and house keys. "You are a sparkle of light in the world." It flashes at me. All I feel when I look at it is shame. I don't live up to this keychain. "Heart," I hear again.

Jamie meets me at the door, takes me into her arms like a mother consoling a child and I cry. Hard. My tears are hot and I can only hope that they have some purpose. I hope that as they stream down my face and onto my sister's strong shoulder that I'm releasing the pain that has been building up, the grief of a relationship lost and the dream of the family I once imagined. Getting rid of the shame that has taken root in me for as long as I can remember. The fear that I will never love again, that I will not have the relationship that I long for. All of it, be gone, I think as I cry harder and harder onto my twin sister. I feel safe in her arms, I'm overwhelmed with gratitude for her.

She is kinder, gentler than me, I think. She is better than me, I think. I'm hurting her by scaring her so she has to come save me in the middle of the night while her family sleeps, I think. I feel like a burden.

In a matter of seconds these thoughts come barging in and take up all the space. No room left for anything else. I whisper into her shoulder, "Thank you, Jamie. I think there is something wrong with my heart."

She takes charge, guiding me to her minivan and opening my door for me and helping me out of the car once we're at the Urgent Care clinic just a few miles away. She takes my insurance card out of my wallet and hands it over the counter to the smiling woman sitting behind the computer.

"Let go," the tattoo on her wrist is in just the right position for me to read it clearly as she types in my name and information. That tingly sensation shoots up my left side and I know that this message is for me and that everything will be OK. I can feel my heart rate slowing and the pain subsiding.

"Amie," a smiling nurse says from the open door to my right. She's wearing blue scrubs and her blond hair is piled on top of her head in a messy bun.

She gets my weight and vitals, asking me a series questions as she pulls out a blue and white patterned gown.

"Go ahead and change into that and I'll be back to start your IV," she instructs, pointing to the neatly folded gown at the end of the bed as she walks out the door.

Jamie takes my clothes from me and I clumsily change into the gown and crawl up on the bed. She grabs a blanket from the counter next to her and puts it over my legs. I pull it up to my shoulders and we wait silently for the nurse.

My IV's started and fluids are pumping into a vein on my left hand.

"I would like to run an EKG and a blood panel to rule out anything serious," Dr. Jones says. He's bald and reminds me a little of Jim Gaffigan. Just taller. I expect him to start telling jokes about bacon but he doesn't. He doesn't seem to have much of a sense of humor at all. All business when he asks me all the serious medical questions, if I have any allergies to medications, symptoms, and then a battery of questions about my symptoms.

"Jane," my nurse finally introduces herself when she comes in to draw my blood. The EKG is done right after and then we wait for Dr. Jones for what seems like an eternity.

"Your blood work came back normal and your EKG shows no signs of cardiac distress," he says looking at his laptop then setting it down on the counter. He sits down on the tiny chrome stool and scoots it closer to my bed.

"Amie, I think you've experienced a panic attack. Have you been under an unusual amount of stress lately?" he asks.

The last few weeks have been stressful, yes, but nothing I can't handle, I think. I'm finding it difficult to adjust to the kids being away twice a week and every other weekend. It feels wrong for them to not be under my roof and I know that I will never get used to this unnatural way of life.

Cal and I stay in touch over WhatsApp. Flirty messages and sweet photos ding throughout my day and make me smile. We have Zoom calls when we can find open time slots that match up to the seven hour time difference.

"I would like to come over on a holiday visa to spend time with you, get acquainted with Colorado," he said on our Zoom call a week ago. I paused too long before answering and I wasn't sure why. I replied something generic like, "That would be nice." But then changed the subject and hung up abruptly to get back to work. "So much to do," I had said. He could feel it, my hesitation, me pulling away. Our conversations have dropped off drastically and a visit hasn't been brought up again.

Oh, and the kids' hedgehog died while they were at their dad's last weekend. We weren't particularly attached to Prickles, but it was a hard loss when I walked down the stairs at noon on a Sunday morning to find his cold prickly body wedged up against his red running wheel, his most prized possession. Gina was in town visiting and she's much braver than me so it was she who picked him up and placed him in a Nike shoebox. Gina is one of my oldest friends. We met freshman year of college and from day one we just got eachother. Of course, she was "our" friend, me and Jamie's. We stayed close when I moved to Denver and even when I went quiet and stopped calling the year I considered betraying my husband and made a decision to bury my doubts and fears, to suck it up. She went through her own struggles with infertility, a premature baby, adoption, and then her own divorce. The bumps of life brought us even closer.

"Amie, it's a hedgehog, throw him in the dumpster and let's go get some damn coffee," she was laughing as I searched my phone for prayers to say over his soul and figure out the right way to dispose of him. I cried — way too much over a hedgehog now that I'm reflecting on it. It somehow made me feel like I failed the kids again. First their parents get a divorce and then their hedgehog dies. The disappointments just kept coming at them.

"No, nothing out of the ordinary," I lie. This is familiar territory. Here I am again, no answer or remedy for my heart pounding out of my chest. No prescription to fill that can keep it from happening again.

Dr. Jones offers me a prescription for Xanax to "take the edge off" in case I have another panic attack. I politely decline and we drive away in Jamie's minivan as the sun rises.

Chapter 19

Recent Searches

- Is five minutes enough time to meditate?
- Is it normal to see colors when you meditate?
- How common is it to see clouds in shape of heart?
- What is a spiritual awakening?

I see black with light poking in and dancing around. My brain strains to see, the light finally taking shape as a silhouette of Mirielle sitting in front of me, one outline of her and then another popping in as the first fades out, over and over again. Her posture the same as mine but much more erect because she's been doing this for decades. Her meditation retreats now a monthly ritual for me, my saving grace as I work hard to keep the panic attacks away.

The leaves are crunchy underneath me, they rustle as I shift around and I can hear the river rushing behind the retreat house. My breath is smooth and quiet as Mirielle instructs, "If thoughts come up, that's OK. Gently focus on the breath and you'll notice that it naturally slows down."

Her silhouette has disappeared. Now there's just black as I look into the back of my eyelids. Thoughts are shooting at me like rapid fire and I can hear the river and the breath of the other 10 people sitting on the silk blankets that are spread across the grass overlooking the zen garden and the river. A boundary from the outside world. A bird is chirping and I hear an airplane above.

"Start with small amounts of time and work your way up," Mirielle reminded me in our last session.

So I do. Every day over the last few weeks. It's part of my new routine to battle the panic attacks that lurk around every corner. I find myself waiting for one to pop up and take my breath away. I sit in excruciating silence looking, searching, hoping for the "space between thoughts" that I was told I would find there in the darkness. I worry that for me there is no space between thoughts. My thoughts are more like a run-on sentence and they keep racing at a rapid speed. When it comes to thoughts, particularly thoughts of worry, I was quite efficient. Very good at the mass number, speed and velocity of thoughts that didn't serve me at all. So I just let them be, left them alone and let them shoot through my brain, spreading like wildfire and not letting up. Yet I stay still this time and let them have me, giving in completely and fully.

I am yet to experience the zen I've read about in books and have heard about from others who frequent these retreats. But today is different.

All is suddenly quiet. The chirping bird is gone. The river has shut off and there is not even a whisper of breath around me. I have either left or I have gone inside myself completely. I don't know but I don't care, it just feels like contentment. There's a flash of blue in the darkness that expands across my closed eyes. It's asking me to go through. I strain to see beyond it, what I might be stepping into but when I try to see past it, the entryway shrinks down. I want to see it desperately so I go back to focusing on my breath, relax my shoulders again and it's back. The blue entryway is growing and through it I see flashes of violet swirling around. I have no idea what any of it means but I feel an overwhelming sense of peace and that I want to sit here forever. I don't even feel my left foot, which I'm sure is numb.

Ding the bell chimes. "When you're ready, bring your focus back to your breath and your awareness back to this physical space," Mirielle sings, her voice quiet and soothing.

I open my eyes and I'm in a new world. The colors are more vivid than they were before I closed my eyes. It's the same scenery but it looks like a painting, the grass around me textured brush strokes of green and brown, the sky swirls of blue and white. My brain strains, looking for its usual list of worries and there is nothing to grasp. My body feels whole, sturdy.

I unfold my legs and step my foot forward into the grass. Every cell of my foot can feel the cool grass underneath, electricity running up through my feet up to my heart. A warm sensation radiates up and settles. I put my hand to my heart and I'm overwhelmed by the feeling of connection to everything in this landscape. This perfect image of what I have known as my world. I feel connected to every blade of grass here and not only can I hear the river rushing again, I can feel it. My heart is in rhythm with the water as it navigates and forces its way through the rocks.

I have never tried a drug in my life but I'm guessing this is what it might feel like to be high or to take ectasy. My brain is trying to rationalize it.

"OK … this can't be real. Maybe my blood sugar is low again. You should get some sugar right away," the neurotic part of my brain warns me. I grab my St. Teresa medallion and thank her. After reading "The Interior Castle," I became quite a fan so I ordered a silver medallion with her delicate face etched on the front and her name on the back. It hangs from a silver chain that I now wear every day. The description on Amazon said, "St. Teresa is the patron saint of body illness and Spanish Catholic Writers." I laughed out loud. Yes, this is the necklace for me, I thought. I also get a kick out of the sheer amount of merchandise with the faces of Saints plastered on them. The Saints are the rockstars of the Catholic community. I no longer consider myself part of that community yet I have adopted some of the amazing learnings from the religion and it has become an important part of who I am. I certainly have an affinity for St. Teresa and without the rigorous education I went through in my twenties, I wouldn't be where I am today.

Where am I today? Spiritually, I've grown and today feels like a tiny glimpse of the joy that lies within when I'm still enough to go beyond my limited beliefs and fear. It's beyond religion. Just like Dr. Knight saying that he will not give me a diagnosis. For the first time in my life I'm unwilling to give myself a label when it comes to something as important as my spirituality. It's unique to me. I came to it and continue to pursue it in the way that works for me and me alone. I see that I'm part of a much bigger community, one where we all belong. If only we're willing to feel it and follow.

I'm a little wobbly but I keep walking toward the river. One slow step at a time, feeling every blade of grass and the soil beneath my feet. The warmth of the sun is beaming down on me, following me like a spotlight as I approach the river bank, my toes inches from the foamy water. I step in carefully, tiptoeing on the smooth rocks peeking up from the shallow water. Then I dig my feet into the coarse sand bed and I let the cold water wash over my feet, the rush of the water spraying up onto my legs and sending a chill up my body.

There is something here that I need to know. I can feel it.

"Look up," I hear. The voice coming from somewhere between my heart and spleen. I drop my head back as far as it will go. The sun is shining so brightly into my eyes that I have to close them for a second. When I open them I nearly lose my balance.

Just above me the clouds are moving rapidly. Within just a few seconds, two clouds collide to form an unmistakable heart. It's big and puffy. No doubt about it, it's clearly a heart in the sky.

"Ha, ha, ha," I squeal with joy. I'm sure I look like a lunatic standing in the river laughing at the sky. *This* is my new normal, I think to myself.

I'm scared to leave. Scared that I'll be unable to bring this magic with me. Scared that once I leave, the peace will be left behind. I sit in my car long after everyone has gone. It's dark, but I can still feel the light all around me.

Chapter 20

Recent Searches

- How to write a Match.com profile
- Sad songs for a gloomy day
- What's a pyre doodle?
- Best kind of food for giant puppies

She charges toward me and in one quick move lands her paws on my shoulders, her fuzzy golden head nuzzles into my shoulder. She licks my face every few seconds and I can't help but giggle like a child. She moves on to Evelyn and Emma, doing the same dance. Her tail is wagging and she's jumping up and down like a rabbit. She's big for a three-month-old puppy, her paws the size of saucers. She's half poodle, half-Pyrenees and she already feels like part of the family.

"Her name is Red," Mark, the breeder says. A little zing in my left leg tells me that this is good.

Red, my grandma's favorite color. Red, my mom's nickname growing up.

I put her in the car. I had no intention of bringing a dog home today but God had another plan so this fluffy golden puppy is riding in my front seat, licking my hand every few minutes.

Even though I've been meditating, praying and keeping the panic attacks away, there's a loneliness that I can't quite shake when the girls are away. Plenty to keep me occupied between work, my writing and my amazing friends, who have been so supportive. Inviting me to happy hours, dinners and yoga classes. But my house feels empty without the kids' backpacks hanging on their hooks in the mud room. No soccer bags, no half drank water glasses on the counter, or dirty socks left in the middle of the room.

The doubt starts to rise up. "What are you doing? You can't make this decision on your own. A dog is a bad idea." But then the doubt disappears when I step outside of my car with Red following and I see a double rainbow. The colors are solid and bright like it's making an especially important statement. The clouds that hung low in the sky all day have stepped out of the way for this magnificent vision.

"No. You need to drop the idea of a dog," the husband would say when I would mentioned it. We had allergies to contend with, but I was hopeful that, one day, the right dog would find its way to us.

We got a puppy just before we were married. Summit was my companion, pure love. She slept next to me every night. When I was pregnant, she followed me everywhere I went, protecting me and was extra gentle. She could sense when I was upset or afraid so she would get closer, stare at me like she was reading my emotions and then promptly nuzzle into my neck, like Red just did, giving me the comfort I needed. At just seven years old she died, hit by a car on a busy street while we were visiting family. I wanted to go to her, tell her goodbye, to hold her paw as she took her last breath, but it was too late. " ... we found her remains on 111th Avenue," the paramedic said when the phone rang 30 minutes after our search for her began.

It was traumatic to lose her this way, so sudden, and I missed the loving spirit she added to our home. I longed for it to be there once again, especially when the kids are away. But for them, too. The love of a pet is pure, a direct access to the Divine in my opinion. I've felt it. As I gaze at her Muppet-looking face and wagging giant tail, I'm struck by the memory of the dog made of light that woke me in the night so many months ago.

Now here she is. Her hair wiry and curly, her nose big and black and her deep brown eyes lined with her shaggy hair that's dangerously close to blocking her vision. She follows me all day and night, whines when I walk out of a room. She's my instant companion, like we've been down this road before. Me leading, her following and the girls her lifelong playmates.

The morning she came home with us the sky was gray, socked in with clouds, a rarity for Colorado. The sky and I were in sync, my mood matched the gloominess. I can't pinpoint one particular thing, more a series of events that left me feeling blah as I went through the motions. I wasn't in the mood to be mindful, it was a day of a list too long to fit the number of hours of daylight, a broken cell phone, clogged toilet and ants scurrying around my kitchen floor. I was overwhelmed so I got myself a Venti Iced Green Tea Latte and drove around in my car for an hour before school pick up. No music on, I talked to God, talked to my angels, and to all the beings who I feel are around me but I can't see. I just chattered away like I would to an old friend, spilling it all.

"… Match.com," announcing the next topic like it was a news headline.

"When Gina was here a few months ago she set up a profile for me and I've had some really great coffee dates. I've dated a couple of very cool men but the whole swiping, liking, winking thing leaves me confused and I somehow feel committed to someone if they buy me a cup of coffee and I don't feel right about dating multiple people, which I believe is the point of online dating, to try people on to see if it's a fit … "

I go on and on with this topic. "Now, how do we feel about this from a spiritual perspective?" I ask. I don't get an answer (from myself) so I keep going, "I wonder if you think I might be lacking in faith if I'm looking online rather than trusting that you will make my life partner appear in Divine time. Or do you work through technology, too? Maybe you impact the matching algorithms?"

Somehow, God and the angels must have concluded that I needed a puppy to fill my time rather than Match.com. I'm in my kitchen making her chicken and rice as the breeder had instructed. " ... she has eggs and bacon on top of her dry food for breakfast," Mark had said when he sent us on our way with a few day's worth of food since I wasn't prepared at all that this day would turn into rainbows and puppies.

Red's finally asleep and so are the girls. The house is quiet but it feels full. I sit down for the first time all day. I took all my conference calls on the run, either walking to the next thing or driving. I haven't had a chance to set up my new phone so I pull it out of the box and enter my passwords, hitting accept when I'm prompted and I let it spin, doing its thing to make all my photos, texts and apps load. This will likely take hours. Although part of me is panicking that I don't have a phone, access to my calendar or the soccer schedules, part of me is relieved to have a little break from this device that is always yelling at me about what's next, what's now, and what I need to be paying attention to.

I check the kids and walk into my bedroom. My closet door is open so I step toward it to close it but something draws me in. I step inside and I have an overwhelming feeling to organize. The plastic bins with purple lids are still full, stacked in the corner. When I moved in I left my closet last, prioritizing it to the bottom of the list. I pulled out the basics, my jeans, favorite shirts and most of my shoes. Some of my jewelry is strung across the long white shelf that lines the back wall. But everything else is untouched, in the same spot the movers placed it a year ago.

One at a time, I pull my clothes, jackets and scarves from the bins. I put some on hangers and fold others neatly and place them on the bright white shelves that line the walls. I color code the hanging clothes and line up my shoes. I pull out my old t-shirts, the ones I've kept for decades as memories of the past. I refold them remembering where I was and how I felt at the times I wore them.

The last bin holds all of the cards I've received, the most recent on top. "Get well soon," "You'll be back on your feet soon," "Thinking of you during this hard time" the cards say in beautiful fonts. All a little different but the sentiment the same. I read the long, loving messages from my family and friends. One from my sister Kate with a bible verse sketched out in her lovely handwriting.

"For I am the Lord your God who takes hold of your right hand and says to you, do not fear; I will help you. – Isaiah 41:13"

This verse carried me through some of the toughest times and continues to be my shield from fear. And the people behind these cards are my greatest cheerleaders. I cry tears of joy as I place the cards in a basket and onto the lowest shelf. All of my belongings now firmly in place in my new home. It finally feels complete.

"Ding" my phone yells at me. I pick it up to google closet organizers but before I can put in my password I see a text notification.

It's from Jonathan, "You ok? Seems like there's something up today."

He has a knack of reaching out at the pivotal times of my life, like he's tapped into my energy field and can sense the shifts. Or maybe he just texts according to the moon cycles and he's way more in tune with how the Universe is impacting me and everyone else. Or maybe he's an alien. I don't know but it freaks me out.

I haven't seen him in more than five years but there is still a connection that is unexplainable. We don't talk but there will be short — yet moving — text exchanges here and there, typically around my breakthroughs and breakdowns, which have been frequent lately. I heard from him the day my divorce was finalized, the night before I flew to see Cal in Ireland, and when I returned from the emergency room.

"I'm great. Big, magical day," I reply and then I take a deep breath.

"Ok," I say, and I hit his phone number. It's ringing. I'm sweating.

"Amie," he sings into my ear, it's clearer on my new, much bigger phone.

"Hi," I breathe, exhaling with the word.

"I just need to ask this question, so I thought I would call," I say without taking a breath.

"Ok, I'll answer," he says slowly.

"Do you plan to get a divorce?"

"No, Amie. My situation hasn't changed and I don't plan on it changing. I am married, but I still have feelings for you and it's just the way it is. I want to keep you in my life, but if that's too hard for you then I understand."

I start to cry; it feels like a loss, but I'm not sure why because it's never belonged to me. I want to hang on, tell him that it's OK, that I will love him, be his friend no matter what his situation is, but I can't. My stomach is flipping, my throat is constricting and I'm aware for the first time that my body is protecting me, telling me what I need to know. We have avoided this topic, tiptoeing around it, but it's the elephant in the room and can't be ignored. He has suggested that we meet for coffee or lunch. I decline every time, waiting for him to offer the information that he's available.

"Jonathan, I am grateful for you. You came into my life and have lifted me up. I want nothing but love, joy and peace for you but I can't continue to participate while you're in a committed relationship. Well, I can. But I won't."

Chapter 21

Recent Searches

- Best beaches in Oahu
- Resort from Forgetting Sarah Marshall movie
- Meaning of Hawaiian leis
- Does natural sunscreen really work?
- Definition of normal

The sand is warm beneath me, my legs folded on top of each other, my hands resting on my knees. I can feel the sun heating up my exposed, bikini-clad skin that's coated with SPF 30. Behind my closed eyes I'm seeing the expanding colors of blue and violet. Then the bizarre happens. There's a download, my life flashing in front of my eyes. But I know that this is not death, instead, a beginning. Moments flashing so rapidly that I'm unable to process even one fully before they disappear and are replaced with the next in rapid succession.

Bright lights, I'm reaching for her hand, pokes in the heel, tubes, crying, then a little older, I'm kicking, giggling, grabbing my toes.

Taller now with pigtails, leg's pumping, wind in my hair on a swing, giggling, a blue blanket, thumb in my mouth watching out the window, wishing.

Then darkness creeps in. Body like concrete, fear rising up and taking over, eyes swollen, head looking down. White dress, a room full of loving faces, first cries, first steps, love, my babies.

I'm lying in bed, there is guilt, shame, sickness and pain. Blood running down my body in the shower, then my mom and dad holding me telling me everything will be OK.

Me in the empty house, curled up on the hardwood floor, tears. Then a burst of brightness, double rainbow, big yellow dog, ring shining on my finger, eagles soaring.

Then, there is nothing. Blank, then the beach scene is painted in front of my eyes. Still, quiet. I see the brushstrokes of the blue sky, the white dabs of foamy waves and the perfect outline of the girls standing with their backs to me, facing the ocean. All the heartache gone, a new scene in front of me.

Their sundresses are lightly blowing in the Hawaiian breeze. No shoes, toes digging into the sand, they exude joy as they let the waves crash over their feet. They're running back and forth between me and the sea, playing with the tide.

We're here on the North Shore of Oahu to celebrate my 41st birthday and to get some rest and relaxation, our first vacation as a family of three.

Five years ago I sat in my closet desperately hanging on to who I wanted to be rather than who I really was. I see now that my connection with Jonathan didn't end my marriage.

It was the shame that I buried. Shame that I could have feelings for a man who is not my husband. But mostly shame that I believed that anyone could have such depth of love for me. I felt unworthy of love.

But it had nothing to do with Jonathan or my husband, not even Cal whom I continue to love from an ocean away. It's all about the ability to love myself. Fully and completely. This is the hardest kind of love I've ever known.

Jonathan and I weren't meant to be together. Admittedly, I spent many years running through the "what ifs" in my mind; lost in the enchantment of a romance that washed all the ugly stuff away. That was certainly an option. But it wasn't the right path for either of us. I was blessed enough to be faced with a man who, like the mysterious light in the middle of the night, tapped me on the shoulder and gave me an opportunity to wake up. It wasn't a call to wake up to a new love, a relationship to replace or fix anything. It was a call to wake up to myself. To the real me, not the people-pleasing me, the fighting-to-be-good-enough me. He held up a mirror and asked me to love myself. I can see that clearly now, but at the time all I could do was look away and bury the mirror deep in that closet.

So began my quest to be fixed. To be normal once again. The definition of normal is conforming to a standard; usual, typical or expected. I'm definitely not normal, not even close to being within normal range. All the blood work and every specialist in the state gave me their best assessments but in those I would never find what I was looking for.

I've decided to create my own chart. One that's big enough for the bigness of me. This new range of measurement is ugly and beautiful. Messy and neat. Happy and sad and often somewhere in between. There is no median to compare. Not for me. Not for anyone.

If I could talk to my younger self just five years ago I would tell her to know that she is good enough just the way she is and no one can take that away. I would say that everything will be OK. All of it. The kids. My health. My marriage. Yes, the marriage ended but it was an important part of my elevation. We always have a choice to rise or fall. I've fallen more than I want to admit but I can say with confidence that although I'm still — and probably always will be — on the rollercoaster, the ride is smoothing out and the journey is a steady incline up.

I didn't expect to survive the emotional rollercoaster of the end of my marriage. I know that the ride isn't over, but I feel stronger now that I'm on the other side of the first big loop. I didn't expect that my body would heal through the process. I've been searching for answers for so long that it became part of who I was. It no longer defines me. The essence of me that bubbled up all those years ago seems to have risen up again and is now too big to shove back down.

I've been guided by what I envision is an army of spiritual warriors. St. Teresa, my grandparents, great grandparents and angels I don't know by name but I know their strength. They continue to send numbers, lovely smells, a whisper, music lyrics that tingle up my left side (which I often mistook for a stroke), dancing lights, visions of dogs and a shiny ring. Now this, all here for my benefit and all guiding me to a beautiful new start.

A fresh lei, a double strand of tuberose and orchids is placed around my neck. It's fragrance strong, a mix of gardenia and lavender fills the air around me. "Happy Birthday," Elizabeth says, kissing me on each cheek. She places one on each of the girls and they smile a shy smile. We're all dressed up for a fancy dinner to celebrate.

When St. Teresa was 41, a priest convinced her to go back to prayer, but she still found it very difficult. She once said, "Prayer is an act of love, words are not needed. Even if sickness distracts from thoughts, all that is needed is the will to love."

The will to love is the only reason I'm here now with my sweet girls and this dear friend in paradise.

"Happy birthday to you, happy birthday to you, happy birthday dear mommy, happy birthday to you."

The candle melting into the crème brulee is flickering as I close my eyes to make a wish.

Printed in the United States
by Baker & Taylor Publisher Services